KOREA
Bilingual Edition

poems by
Han-Jae Lee

translated by
Jae-Mo Lee

River Sanctuary
PUBLISHING

Felton, CA

Korea Bilingual Edition

ISBN 978-1-952194-04-7

Printed in the United States of America

ACKNOWLEDGMENTS

The author would like to thank the editors of the following publications in which these poems have appeared, some in earlier versions:

Caesura: "Invisible Leash"
Crab Orchard Review: "Wasted Tire"
Catamaran Literary Reader: "Cobweb"
Monterey Poetry Review: "Flower Watch," "The Sorrow"
Sand Hill Review: "Secluded Life," "Times Square," "Pedestrian Crosswalk at Times Square"
PCC Inscape Magazine: "Heavy Rain Showers"
Military Experience & The Arts: "Outside the National Cemetery"
Snapdragon Journal: "The Snail"
EMRYS Journal: "Magnolia"

Special thanks to my beloved family and friends who gave me support and encouragement during the writing of this book.

And gratitude to all of my teachers and poets who helped me to shape these poems: Alexander E. Braun, Barbara Beswetherick, Judy Bernstein, Yvonne Cannon, Magdalena Montagne, Jennifer Franklin, Gillian Cumming, Kenneth Share, Aubrey Moncrieffe, Rosanne English, Gi- Taek Kim, Yeung-Nam Kim, Su-Ik Lee, and others too numerous to name.

Cover Photography: Jeong-Soo Lee
Author Photo: Mike Seungwook Lee

River Sanctuary Publishing
P.O. Box 1561
Felton, CA 95018
www.riversanctuarypublishing.com
also available on Amazon.com

KOREA

Table of Contents

I.

II.

III.

IV.

for my dear family

I.

Korea My Homeland

Korea! My native land!
Just hearing the name makes my heart flutter.

How long I have lived away from my native country!
Even though I can never forget it in my dreaming.

My homeland in the Far East.
This pleasant country where my ancestors dwelled for thousands of years.

A free country defended from the invasions of foreign nations.
In the ruins of war bloomed the rose of freedom.

Where the sun first comes up on the continent.
Where there are four seasons.

In March the countryside feels the start of spring.
My rural home with its rocks and hills.

The peaches and apricots in full bloom.
The breezes blowing soft and fresh.

Though time and tides flow away,
spring, summer, autumn and winter will return there
again and again.

Are my childhood friends still living there, I wonder?
Even though I am far away from my home
this yearning makes me grow fonder.

Loving this land where cherished dreams are realized.
I would like to mount up to the sky like a huge white crane
and see Korea again.

코리아 나의 조국

이름만 들어도 가슴 설레는
나의 조국 코리아

꿈에도 잊을 수 없는 조국을
떠나와 산 지 몇 해던가

극동에 있는 나의 조국
조상들이 수천 년 살아온 곳

무수한 외세의 침략을 물리쳐
자유를 지켰고 전쟁의 폐허에서
장미꽃을 피운 곳

대륙에서 해가 맨 처음 뜨고
사계절이 있는 곳

3월에 들판에 봄기운이 시작되면
고향의 바위틈과 언덕에서 봄이 싹트고

배꽃과 살구꽃이 활짝 피고
부드럽고 향기로운 봄바람이 부는 곳

세월이 가도 봄 여름 가을 겨울
사계절이 변함없이 찾아주는 곳

유년의 친구들은 아직 그곳에 살고 있을까?
고향을 멀리 떠나와 있어도
그리움은 갈수록 깊어만 간다

품은 꿈을 이룰 수 있는 곳
커다란 백학이 되어 하늘 높이 날아올라
그리운 고국을 다시 보고 싶다

San Francisco

My friend, you will see the seashore
where the splendid blue sky
pours down its pails of glaring sunlight;
nearby ridges beckoning to come
on wings of fresh green foliage.

Where often chilly wind
wafts in from the Pacific;
this is San Francisco.

When you come here, my friend
you will find the Golden Gate Bridge
the pink of cherry blossoms
connecting north and south.

We could lounge on Baker Beach.
And at Fisherman's Wharf we could cook the entire coastline!
At the Gold Dust Lounge we'll drink and dance.

We could place our chairs facing the waves on the beach
and see a myriad of stars in the brilliant night sky
as we raise our eyes heavenward.

The fatigue of a long journey of flowing life behind us
we see a crowd,
a host of yellow daffodils,
fluttering and dancing alongside the beach
like the women we might meet.

샌프란시스코

해변에는 새파란 하늘이
눈부신 햇살을 양동이로 퍼붓고
신록의 날개 옷을 입은 산들은
이리 오너라 손짓을 하며

태평양에서 시원한 바람이
자주 불어오는 곳
친구야, 이곳은 샌프란시스코

친구야, 이곳에 오면
남과 북을 잇는 복사꽃 분홍색
금문교를 보게 될 거야

우리는 함께 베이커 해변을 거닐 수 있고
피셔맨 부두에서는 어디서나
파티를 즐길 수 있을 거야
그리고 골드 더스트 라운지에서
술 한 잔하고 춤을 추세

해변에 의자를 갖다 놓고
파도를 바라볼 수 있을 것이고
눈을 들어 찬란한 밤하늘의
무수한 별들을 볼 수도 있겠지

흐르는 인생의 긴 여행에서 오는
피곤함을 뒤로하면
해안을 따라 수많은 노란 수선화들이
우리가 만나는 여인들처럼
흔들리며 춤추는 걸 볼 수 있을 거야

Another World

I talked about the past with people I did not know
who looked like they came from dreams.

Their faces seemed picturesque
like the surface of meandering streams.
Their voices were a gentle breeze.

We walked along the village road—
the wildflowers in full bloom,
downy clouds dotting the sky.

Then, like an illusion
these strangers passed through the flowers
one by one.

I stopped walking and took a closer look at the flowers
comprised entirely of diverse unknowns.
Each one having its own life and universe.

After all the people were gone
I could only see myself.
A man who stood behind me.

또 다른 세상

꿈속에서 본 듯한
낯선 사람들과 대화를 했다

겉모습은 굽이쳐 흐르는 냇물 같았고
목소리는 부드러운 봄바람 같았다

야생화가 만개하고
하늘에는 솜털구름이 흩어져 있는
시골길을 함께 걸었다

걷던 도중 그 사람들은 마치 환상처럼
하나둘씩 꽃들 사이로 사라지기 시작했다

걸음을 멈추고 그들이 사라진 꽃들을
유심히 살펴보니 미지의 여러 꽃들은
각자의 생명과 우주를 품고 있었다

사람들이 모두 꽃들 사이로 사라지고
남은 사람은 내 등 뒤에 서있던 사람
나 혼자 뿐이었다

Wet Fog

Wet fog comes frequently to Daly City.
Looks like fog the fine trees seem to murmur.
Wet fog blows up from the coast side of the Pacific.

Like the huge white cranes
whose wings spread throughout the city and one after another
suck up the parks, houses, streets, and people.

Wet fog doesn't talk all day long
and when the sunlight breaks through
returns to a far-off shore.

During its stay in the city
wet fog doesn't hurt even a petal or a dog.
Wet fog walks softly, laughing without sound, smiling…

Wishing to make friends with people
wet fog drops inside houses,
participates in parties and disappears.

When wet fog feels ennui it rises quickly and becomes the ridges of waves.
When it wishes to hear the sound of water
wet fog becomes the drizzling rain.

물안개

물안개는 자주 달리 시를 찾는다
태평양 연안에서 오는 물안개 속에서
소나무들은 작은 소리로 속삭이는 듯

물안개는 도시를 모두 덮어버리는
거대한 백학의 날개처럼
공원과 집들과 거리와 사람들을
하나둘씩 삼켜버린다

물안개는 종일 침묵하다가
햇빛이 나면 먼 바다로 돌아간다

물안개는 도시에 머무는 동안
꽃잎 하나 개 한 마리 해치지 않는다
소리 없이 웃고 미소 지으며 걷는다

물안개는 사람들과 친구가 되기 위해
집안에 들어가 파티에 참석한 후 사라진다

물안개는 권태로우면 재빨리 일어나
산더미 같은 파도로 변하고
물소리가 그리우면 보슬비가 된다

By the Golden Gate Bridge

After the fog lifts—a beautiful morning calm.
The broad sun comes up as usual.

The gentleness of heaven is on this bridge.
A massive structure of pink.

The bridge appears magnificent.
Wearing the beauty of the morning silently.
The blue sky overhead, bright and glittering.

Many visitors pass over the bridge
from many countries.
Whole generations.

The travel guide for San Francisco claims:
*The earth hasn't anything to show more stately and beautiful
than the Golden Gate Bridge.*

Perhaps it is this brilliance that causes
the impulse to jump into the waters below.

The loveliness of the bridge tarnished
by sadness and solemnity.

Above the blue and windy sea
the sun shines on the bridge.

금문교에서

안개가 걷힌 후 아름다운 아침의 고요
평소처럼 태양이 밝게 빛나고

천상의 부드러움이 금문교에 드리워지는
핑크 빛 거대한 구조물

아름다운 아침에
금문교의 모습은 장엄하다

푸른 하늘은 밝게 빛나고
많은 나라에서 온 모든 세대의
방문객들이 금문교를 지나간다

샌프란시스코 여행가이드는
"지구상에 금문교보다 더 장엄하고
아름다운 것은 없다" 라고 말한다

이 찬란함이 금문교 아래로
뛰어내리고 싶은 충동을 불러일으킨다

금문교의 아름다움은
슬픔과 침통함으로 인해 그 빛을 잃었다

바람 부는 푸른 바다 위 금문교에
태양이 밝게 빛난다

On the Muni Bus in San Francisco

Rush hour is always crowded on the Metro.
More passengers are standing than sitting—
not even comprehending this inconvenience.

Along the route an electric signal
continuously informs travelers of the next stop
and the next.

On Monday mornings some people doze.
Someone gurgles with a cold.
A teenage boy, wearing headphones, laughs, while watching his mobile phone.

It seems the passengers have deep monologues inwardly.
But no one converses with each other.
Only an awkward silence hangs over them.

Perhaps they understand—
like a drunkard, or a farmer, returning to his grass hut in the late afternoon—
that to live is to keep silent.

At intervals, an elderly grandmother
coughs with a choking sound.
The passengers avert their eyes, closing them, or looking out the window.

Even when a disabled old man boards in a wheelchair
they stand aside for him
in silence.

While the Muni bus carries this tough life slowly
I recall nostalgic moments of bygone days
and hurl a handful of tears at the window.

In moments of reverie, I miss my stop.
Firmly grasping the call line to get off.

샌프란시스코 버스에서

출퇴근 시간 버스는 항상 붐빈다
앉은 사람들보다 더 많은 사람들이
불편함을 의식하지 않고 서서 간다

전기신호가 전 구간에 걸쳐 쉬지 않고 승객들에게
다음 정거장과 그 다음 정거장을 알려주고 있다

일부 승객들은 월요일 아침처럼 졸고 있다
한 사람은 감기 때문에 콜록거리고
헤드폰을 낀 십대소년은 휴대폰을 보며 웃고 있다

승객들은 속으로 깊은 독백을 하고 있는 것 같다
서로 대화를 하지 않으니 어색한 침묵만이 흐른다

아마도 그들은 알고 있을 것이다,
술꾼이나 늦은 오후에 오두막집으로 돌아가는 농부처럼
산다는 것은 침묵한다는 것을

할머니 한 분이 숨이 막히는 듯 간간히 기침을 한다
승객들은 외면하거나 눈을 감거나 창밖을 내다보고 있다

장애 할아버지 한 분이 휠체어를 타고 버스에 오를 때도
승객들은 조용히 비켜 주기만 한다

버스가 힘든 삶을 천천히 이동시켜주는 동안
나는 옛 향수에 젖어 한 줌의 눈물을 유리창에 뿌린다

상념에 잠겨 있다가 내려야 할 정거장을 놓치고
하차를 위한 호출 선을 단단히 당긴다

At the Subway

At the Powell station of the BART
in San Francisco
I see a foreigner carrying a heavy bag.

He asks me the way,
pointing to the subway map with his finger.
He seems to know no English.

When he speaks with embarrassment, I can't understand.
It looks like he is pointing to the symbol for the airport.
I can tell by his body language that he worries that he will miss his plane.

Suddenly I recall the days
when I didn't know my way on the subway
and puzzled over what to do.

It was not easy to explain to him
with gestures and movements
that the airport train would be arriving at the station shortly.

I watched him
as he tried to catch the train that was going the wrong way.
Knowing he was not going to get on the airport train.

His harried actions only made things more difficult for him.
His fingers moved faster as he talked to another stranger.
Groans came out of his mouth unconsciously.

There was no one to restrain his actions;
and not only the hour of the airplane's departure
seemed to be accelerating.

지하철에서

샌프란시스코 바트 파월정거장에서
외국인 한 사람이 무거운 가방을 메고 가는 걸 본다

그는 손가락으로 지하철 지도를 가리키며 길을 묻는다
영어를 전혀 모르는 것 같다

그가 내게 말을 걸지만 나는 그가 무슨 말을 하는지
알아들을 수 없다 그가 공항표시를 가리키는 것 같다
그의 손짓 발짓을 보니 비행기를 놓칠까 봐 걱정하는 것
같다

갑자기 나는 내 자신이 지하철에서 어디로 갈지 몰라
당황했던 시절이 생각난다

그에게 손짓 발짓으로 공항 열차가 역에 곧 도착할 거라고
설명하기가 쉽지 않았다

나는 그가 공항과는 반대 방향으로 가는 열차를 타려는 걸
바라보고 그가 공항 열차를 타지 못할 것을 알게 되지만

안절부절하는 그의 행동이 상황을 더 어렵게 만들 뿐
다른 사람과 말할 때 그의 손가락들은 더 빨리 움직이고
있었다
그의 입에서 탄식이 무의식적으로 터져 나왔다

그의 행동을 저지하는 사람은 아무도 없었다
가속페달을 밟고 있는 것은
비행기 출발시간만이 아닌 것 같았다

Spring Days' Rebellion

After frequently exchanging whispers
among the haze, breeze and sunshine of spring
this upheaval begins without notice.

At first this rebellion seems to be insignificant
but the days go by, the signs come from here and there,
and the weeds quickly spread through gardens, fields and streams.

Pushing the hard surface of the earth
the fresh green sprouts ascend from the soil;
there is no Maginot Line against them.

Yesterday's roads cast off their skin
and stirring from sleep the withering branches wriggle.
Rutting bamboo buds jump up from their roots.

The rebellion is pleasant all around
and the cheerful uprising is continued
until the coming brilliance of summer.

Although the woods suffered last winter,
the fallen leaves here and there joyfully sing for the coming days;
forsythias open their eyes to see the green fields.

The aching remembrance of past seasons is not forgotten.
But the fragrance of the flowers tempt the bees to go out into the
fields and the tender smile of the southern breeze beckons.

봄날의 반란

봄날 아지랑이와 산들바람과 햇빛이
서로 빈번하게 속삭이더니
예고도 없이 반란을 일으킨다

처음에는 이 반란이 별 게 아닌 것 같더니
며칠 지나가자 여기저기서 조짐이 나타나
정원이며 들판이며 시냇가 할 것 없이
푸른 풀이 순식간에 점령해버린다

신록들이 땅속에서 대지의 단단한 표면을 뚫고 나오니
이들을 저지할 수 있는 마지노선은 없다

길은 어제까지의 허물을 벗고
움츠렸던 나뭇가지들은 잠에서 깨어 꿈틀거리고
발정 난 죽순은 뿌리에서 솟아오른다

사방에서 일어나는 이 반란은
눈부신 여름이 올 때까지 즐겁게 진행되리라

숲은 지난겨울 고난을 겪었지만
여기저기 흩어진 낙엽들은
다가오는 날들을 반기는 노래를 부르고
개나리는 푸른 들판을 보려고 눈을 뜬다

지난 계절의 아픈 기억은 잊히지 않아도
꽃의 향기는 벌들로 하여금 들로 가게하고
남풍은 부드러운 미소로 손짓을 한다

Welcome Spring

You, my lover of spring, who has returned to me.
Please give me the chance to embrace you again.
For I am penitent after my foolishness.

Yearning like an orphan who has lost his parents.
Hugging my heart.
My lover of spring.

Please help me recover the burning passion
that has cooled in your absence.
Let your warm smile sprout blossoms that have withered away.

You, my lover of spring,
I never groaned or complained of any discomfort
while I waited for you.

Let's enjoy a picnic under the cherry blossoms.
Let's sing in chorus.
Welcome spring!

You, my lover of spring, who has come back again.
Let's go together and not separate again.

봄맞이

내게 다시 돌아온 그대 내 사랑 봄이여
나의 어리석음을 뉘우치고 있나니
다시 한 번 그대를 내 품에 안게 해다오

나의 사랑 봄이여
부모를 잃은 어린애처럼 가슴을 부둥켜안고
그대를 그리워했노라

그대가 없는 동안 차갑게 식어버린
나의 불타던 정열을 되찾게 해다오
그대의 따스한 미소로 시들어버린 꽃들을 싹트게 해다오

그대 내 사랑 봄이여
그대를 기다리는 동안 나는 한 번도
그대가 없다는 이유로 끙끙대거나 불평하지 않았노라

반가운 내 사랑 봄이여
벚꽃나무 밑에서 소풍을 즐기며
함께 노래를 부르자

다시 돌아온 그대 내 사랑 봄이여
다시는 헤어지지 말고 함께 나아가자

Whispers of Spring

I open the window suddenly,
believing I hear
last year's fallen leaves
rustling in the wind.
But they are not there.

Instead, I hear whispers
from the yellow sprouts
of forsythia in the
garden.
Buds just forming
from thin branches.
Perhaps the yellow color of buds
call and halt me.

In the park—branches of white magnolias in full bloom,
red azaleas and pink cherry blossoms
moving in the breeze.
Their flowers come early,
before their leaves.

Messengers of the season, they knock.
First to awaken spring!
Bringing the light of the sun.
Causing the streams to flow.
Singing a song that twittering birds join.
Forcefully launching a fresh spring.

These messengers tell me that spring has come.
But will vanish without much notice.

봄의 속삭임

작년에 떨어진 낙엽이
바람에 바스락대는 것 같아
문득 창문을 열어보니 낙엽은 보이지 않고
정원의 개나리 노란 싹들의 속삼임이 들린다

가느다란 가지에 금방 맺힌
노란 봉오리들이
나를 불러 멈추게 하는 것 같다

공원에는 잎보다 먼저 피는 목련꽃이
활짝 피었고 붉은 진달래와 분홍 벚꽃이
바람에 흔들리고 있다

봄의 전령들은 먼저 봄을 노크해 깨우고
햇빛을 데려오고 개울물을 흐르게 하고
노래를 부르며 새봄을 이끌어 전진한다

이 전령들은 나에게 봄이 왔음을 알리지만
별다른 예고도 없이 떠나갈 것이다

Cherry Blossoms

During the cherry blossom festival
pale pink flowers cover the entire sky.

Laughing and waving their hands
they gladly greet me.

Their sunny smiles and fresh smells
wash away the fatigue of daily life.

It's like a beauty contest
with musical instruments in a schoolgirls' band.

The flowers are singing songs all along
and even dancing in the breeze.

With all the flowers so similar
how do I choose the most beautiful?

Looking more closely, I see that, like the faces of people,
the countenances of the flowers are different.

Similarly, we may be seen as the same person by the flowers.
They have their own universe; embrace sunshine, dew, wind and sky
as they blossom uniquely.

How long will the festival of ecstasy continue?
Can they know the way to eternal joy?

Desires toward what is beautiful
may lead us endlessly.

벚꽃

벚꽃 축제 중에는
연분홍 꽃들이 하늘을 가린다

꽃들이 손을 흔들어
인사를 하며 나를 반긴다

꽃들은 밝은 미소와 상큼한 향기로
내 일상의 고단함을 씻어낸다

꽃의 향연은 여학생 밴드부가
연주하는 미인대회 같다

꽃들은 축제동안
노래를 부르며 춤을 춘다

비슷하게 생긴 모든 꽃 중에서
가장 예쁜 꽃을 어떻게 고를까

자세히 보니 꽃들의 모습이
사람 얼굴처럼 서로 다르다

마찬가지로 꽃들에게는 사람들이
모두 똑같아 보일 것이다
그들에게도 그들만의 우주가 있어
각자 피어나며 햇빛과 이슬과
하늘을 받아들일 것이다

황홀함의 축제는 얼마나 계속될까
꽃들도 한없는 기쁨을 알고있을까

아름다움을 추구하는 욕망은
우리를 영원히 이끌어 줄 것이다

Toward the End of Cherry Picking Season

Monday morning
after a weekend full of pickers.
Toward the end of cherry picking season.

All the lovely guests had come together
like the inflow of tides.

Taking joyfully the fresh and virgin cherries.
Until fully satisfied.

Now gone as tide ebbs.
Only a few cherries
hang lonely on the trees.

In order to be loved
the cherries waited a long time.
Together with the farmer from the beginning of spring.

The sky darkened with clouds and
peals of thunder were heard frequently.
The cherries brightened their bodies
with deep red lipstick.

The harmony of the cherries' colors and their dreams
at last fulfilled
by those who picked them.

체리 수확이 끝나갈 무렵

체리 수확이 끝나갈 무렵
주말에 체리 따는 사람들이
몰려왔다 떠나간 월요일 아침

사랑스러운 방문객들이
밀물처럼 한꺼번에 몰려와

순결하고 신선한 체리를 만족할 만큼
즐거운 마음으로 수확해 갔다

썰물 지나간 자리처럼
몇 개의 체리들이 외로이 나무에 남아있다

체리들은 사랑받기 위해
농부들과 함께 초봄부터 오랫동안 기다렸다

하늘에는 먹구름이 덮였고
천둥소리가 수시로 들렸다
진홍색 립스틱처럼
체리들은 밝게 빛났다

사람들이 체리를 수확하니 체리의 색깔과
꿈의 조화가 마침내 완성되었다

Watermelon

She relaxes with a smile.
In joy and sorrow she welcomes all people
with looks of delight.

Her disposition is that of a good-natured person.
Though her external features have well-rounded
corners her heart is filled with sharp passions.

Her nature is to help others.
She gives willingly of herself
to those who are thirsty.

Reminds them not to swallow
the seeds,
while taking her flesh.

수박

그녀는 미소를 지으며 쉬고 있다
기쁠 때나 슬플 때도
모든 사람을 반갑게 맞는다

그녀는 착한 성품으로
겉모습은 둥그렇지만
속은 강력한 정열로 꽉 차있다

그녀는 천성적으로 남을 도우며
목마른 사람에게는
기꺼이 자신을 내어준다

사람들이 수박을 먹을 때
씨는 삼키지 말 것을 일깨워 준다

Morning Glory

Turning the corner in front of my house
a purple morning glory seems to beckon.
But I can't stop for her
or I'll be late for work again.

Even though I can see through the gaps in the fence
that she is blooming brightly
in the morning sunlight and dewy grasses
I cannot stop now.

She looks unwilling though to have me take leave.
Even bows down to me in the breeze.
I thought I would have time to love her
when I returned later.

However, she did not wait for me.

Though she had looked so gorgeous earlier
by the time I went back
in late afternoon
she had faded.

나팔꽃

집 앞 모퉁이를 도니
자줏빛 나팔꽃 한 송이가
손짓을 해도
발을 멈추면 출근이 늦어져
그럴 수가 없네

이슬 젖은 풀 속에서
아침햇살을 받고
밝게 피어나는 나팔꽃
울타리의 틈 사이로 보이지만
나는 멈출 수 없네

나팔꽃은 나를 떠나보내기 싫은 듯
산들바람 속에 나를 향해
고개 숙여 인사를 하네
나중에 시간을 내 다시 돌아와
사랑해 주리라 생각했는데

그러나 그녀는
기다려 주지 않았네

아침에 그렇게도 아름다웠던 나팔꽃
늦은 오후에 돌아오니 시들어 있었네

Dandelion

One yellow dandelion blooms
alone by the fence.

On the other side
people are busy coming and going.

The dandelion flower seems to have much curiosity about these people
and tries to lean toward the pedestrians.

But the dandelion leaf worries that someone will tread on the flower.
The leaf makes an effort to hold the petals back, so they do not lean.

The fence also exerts pressure on the flower—
holding her back.

The breeze blows over in the leaf's direction
trying to help the leaf stall the dandelion's progress.

Spring noon's sunshine falls in snatches around the pedestrians
creating power for the leaf through photosynthesis.

The dandelion, smaller than the other flowers,
is perhaps curious about tall things.

Eventually this curiosity turned into spores and dispersed in the air.
Then white dandelion seeds wandered away.

Riding the wind
flying fast to the end of the sky.

민들레

노란 민들레 한 송이가 울타리 옆에 외로이 피어있네
울타리 반대편에는 사람들이 바쁘게 오가고 있네

민들레 꽃은 지나가는 사람들에게 관심이 많은지
행인들을 향해 몸을 기울이고 있네

민들레 잎은 누군가에게 밟히지 않을까 걱정을 하네
잎은 꽃잎들이 기울지 않도록 보호하려고 애를 쓰네

울타리 역시 힘을 가해 꽃을 저지하고

산들바람은 잎의 방향으로 불어와
민들레가 앞으로 나가지 못하도록 잎을 도와주네

행인들이 오가는 길목에서 잎은 봄날 오후의 햇빛을 받아
광합성으로 에너지를 주고 있네

다른 꽃들보다 작은 민들레는 키가 큰 것들에 대해
호기심이 있는 듯

이 호기심은 포자로 변해 허공으로 흩어지고
하얀 민들레 씨는 바람을 타고 하늘 끝까지 날아간다

Cobweb

A spider, all alone, is building a cobweb in the corner of the hamlet.
His house waves in the breeze, shaded by a drift of clouds.

Though it is only sounds and sunshine that he hauls up,
he mends the net strand by strand, as if according to musical notation.

Which line has to be installed first or last? How long?
He is a skilled carpenter, humming to himself as he builds.

"What stays where the winds have passed?"
"How long will I have to wait?"

Though it is only a shadow in the moonlight and on the morning dew,
he is never giving up on his house.

He continues to inhabit the garden
where the sparrows twitter and the children chatter.

The spider is conceiving a dream of a loving nest
within the cosmos that hugs the sky, villages and byways.

거미집

거미 한 마리가 시골 마을 한 구석에 혼자 거미집을 짓고 있다
거미집은 미풍에 흔들리고 흘러가는 구름에도 그림자 진다

거미줄에 걸리는 것은 단지 잡소리와 햇빛뿐이지만
거미는 악보에 음표를 써가듯 한 가닥 한 가닥씩 집을 지어간다

어느 줄을 먼저 설치하고 어느 줄을 나중에 설치할까?
얼마나 길게 할까?
콧노래를 부르며 집을 짓는 거미는 숙련된 목수다

"바람이 지나가고 난 다음에는 무엇이 남지?"
"얼마나 오랫동안 기다려야 하지?"

집은 비록 달빛 아래 희미하고
아침이슬에 맺힌 그림자에 불과할지라도
거미는 결코 자신의 집 짓는 일을 멈추지 않는다

거미는 참새들이 지저귀고 어린 애들이 재잘대는
정원에 살고 있다

거미는 푸른 하늘과 동네와 오솔길이 어우러진 세상에서
자신이 좋아하는 집을 지으며 오늘도 꿈을 꾸며 살고있다

Cradle Song

Chirr! Chi—rr! Chirr! Chi—rr!
The cicadas sing again in my backyard, signaling the summer season.
A refrain that happens each night and day.

The song begins with a single cicada
but soon a number of insects are chirring together.
Lazily they sing, without doing any work like the industrious bees.

Listening long enough I hear a pattern in the chirring
and I try to view their chirrs as a delightful chorus of rural life.
But I hear the sound differently according to my mood.

When I feel comfortable after a meal, the intonation is a cradle song.
But after a day filled with annoyances, it becomes a bothersome noise
like the sound of someone weeping.

자장가

맴맴맴맴, 여름 매미가
뒷마당에서 또 운다
밤낮 반복해 울고 있다

처음에 한 마리가 울기 시작하면
이내 여러 마리가 따라서 운다
벌들처럼 부지런히 일하지 않고
게으른 매미들은 노래만 부른다

매미소리를 오래 들으니 그 속에
한 가지 패턴이 있어 시골의 삶을
찬미하는 합창이라 여기고 싶지만
내 기분에 따라 다르게도 들린다

식사를 한 후 기분이 좋을 때면
매미소리는 자장가처럼 들리지만
짜증스럽기 만한 하루가 끝날 무렵에는
사람울음처럼 귀찮은 소음으로 들린다

Evening Primrose

In summertime, the evening primrose
opens her yellow flowers
when the sun retires.

Because of loving the stars
she opens anew her exquisite blossoms
when night falls.

Because of loving the moon
the primrose blossoms alone
contrary to most of the other flowers
blooming only in daylight hours.

When the crescent moon appears
the primrose tells whimsical stories until dawn.
When the moon is full
she delights in animated conversation.

When there is no moon
she converses with the myriad stars and galaxies
in the brilliant night sky
about the mythologies of the constellations.

달맞이꽃

달맞이꽃은
여름 해질녘에 핀다

달맞이꽃은
별을 사랑하기에
밤이 올 때
아름답게 피어난다

달맞이꽃은
달을 사랑하기에
낮 시간에만 피는
다른 꽃들과는 반대로
밤에만 홀로 핀다

초승달이 뜨면
달맞이꽃은 새벽까지
재미있는 이야기를 하고
보름달이 뜨면
활기찬 대화를 즐긴다

달이 뜨지 않으면
달맞이꽃은 무수한 별들과
밤하늘에 밝게 빛나는 은하와
여러 별자리들의 신화에 대한
대화를 나눈다

Lilacs Bloom Again

Lilacs bloom again.
Lilacs bloom again.
Light purple lilacs bloom again
by the grave of my love.

Spring has come again.
Spring breezes have blown in again.

Once I thought that the memory of our first kiss
under the lilac bush in the evening
and the solemn vow
like golden flowers
would vanish like a breeze
and be gone completely.

I made every effort to erase these memories, but in vain.
Now lilacs awaken within me the forgotten faint fragrance
and her warm breath.
Her bright smile
revealed by the lilac.

At first I hated these lilacs.
Forgotten love,
Unforgettable love.
She comes with the lilacs and vanishes silently.

Alas! I would never send her away.
And I call her name repeatedly.
Only my sorrow and sighing echoes into air.
Lilacs bloom again.

라일락 꽃이 다시 피네

라일락이 다시 피네
라일락이 다시 피네
연자줏빛 라일락이
연인의 무덤가에 다시 피네

새봄이 왔네
봄바람이 또 불어오네

나는 한때 생각했지
그날 저녁 라일락 숲에서의 첫 키스의 추억과 황금꽃 같은
우리의 굳은 맹세는 바람처럼 사라져 없어질 거라고
그 추억을 지워버리려 무척 애썼지만 지울 수 없었네

라일락 꽃을 보니 그간 잊었던
그녀의 희미한 향기와 숨결이 떠오르네
라일락 꽃을 닮은 그녀의 빛나는 미소

처음에 나는 라일락 꽃을 싫어했지
잃어버린 연인, 잊을 수 없는 연인,
그녀는 라일락과 함께 왔다 조용히 사라지네

아, 지금이라면 그녀를 결코 보내지 않을 텐데
그녀의 이름을 부르고 또 불러보지만
슬픈 탄식만이 허공에 메아리 칠 뿐

Magnolia

Just when I am getting into my car
someone seems to call to me.
I look back hastily.

I see my mother wearing white clothes
and smiling brightly
beyond the gate of the cemetery.

I return to her
as she waves both hands emphatically
crying out to me:

*"Oh no, no, you are too late to come back to your home,
and you should not drive too fast on this road."*

When I look again where she last stood
the magnolia tree with its white blossoms
is swaying in the breeze.

목련꽃

차를 막 타려고 하는 데 누가 나를 부르는 것 같아
급히 뒤돌아본다

어머니가 묘지 입구 건너편에서 하얀 옷을 입고
환하게 웃고 계신다

나는 급히 어머니에게 되돌아간다
그러자 어머니는 두 손을 힘차게 저으시며 말씀하신다

　"안 된다. 네 집에 돌아가기엔 너무 늦었다.
가는 길에 과속하지 마라."

어머니가 서 계신 자리를 다시 보니
하얀 목련 꽃이 미풍에 흔들리고 있다

Apple Memories

At Hillview Farm each fall
apples hang in clusters
on the branches appetizingly.

I pick the ripe red apples,
filling basket after basket.
My children looking on.

More than the red fruit in my hands
these apples are made up of blue skies, water and wind
and pleasing sunshine.

After awhile the cheeks of the apples
look like the glowing cheeks
of my smiling children—
laughing happily
gathering up the fruit
scooping them into baskets.

And the apples also
seem to be laughing.

Do the apples keep these memories for a long time, I wonder? Cher-
ishing the fragrant air, released willingly,
selflessly shared year after year.

Do the apples treasure
the bright smiles of my children,
happily as their own?

사과에 대한 추억

매년 가을에 힐뷰농장
사과나무가지마다
사과가 탐스럽게 열린다

빨갛게 익은 사과를 따
여러 바구니를 채우는 걸
내 아이들이 바라본다

내 손에 들어있는 이 붉은 과일들은
푸른 하늘과 물과 바람과
상쾌한 햇빛으로 만들어진 것

사과를 따 바구니에 담으면
행복하게 웃음 짓는 내 아이들의 발그스레
상기된 두 뺨 같아 보이기도하고
아이들과 함께 웃고 있는 것 같기도 하다

사과는 해마다 향기를 소중히 간직했다가
사람들을 위해 헌신적으로 내주었던
자신의 추억을 오래 간직할까

사과는 내 아이들의 밝은 미소를
그들의 것인 양 행복하게 간직할까

April

April's cold claws still remain in places
and the winds in the alley
still blow harshly.

On the sunny side of the street a cat yawns.
Grinning from ear to ear it stretches out its front paws.
His protruding tongue lengthens to bathe its body, even its tail.
The helpful breeze licks, smooths down its fur.

The forsythia blooms its diminutive yellow petals.
A broody hen broods over her chicks.
One curious hatchling tries to climb onto its mother's back
slips down again and again.

Tree boughs stretch their bodies.
Their branches saturated by the spring haze.
Breezes extend their height long into the sky.

4월

4월의 차가운 발톱은 곳곳에 남아있다
그래서 때로는 골목길에 세찬 바람이 분다

도로변 양지 바른 곳에서 고양이가 하품을 한다
양쪽 귀가 닿도록 웃으며 앞발을 쭉 편다
혀를 길게 빼 몸부터 꼬리까지 핥는다
봄바람이 도와주려는 듯 고양이 털을
부드럽게 눕혀준다

노란 개나리 작은 꽃잎들이 피어나고
암탉은 병아리들을 품고 있는데
호기심 많은 병아리 한 마리가
어미 닭 등으로 기어오르다 자꾸만 미끄러진다

쭉 뻗은 큰 나뭇가지에서 퍼져 나온
작은 나뭇가지들을 봄 안개가 흠뻑 적시고 있다
봄바람 속에 나뭇가지들은
하늘을 향해 쭉쭉 뻗어 나간다

Coaxing the Buds into Flower

On my wife's birthday, I bought her a bouquet,
pink flowers in a white porcelain vase—
five lilies, five tulips, five roses.
Only the five lilies were not yet flowering.

But I was hopeful
the buds would burst
into blossom soon.

Each day I changed the water in the vase
and trimmed the bottom stems a little
to coax them into flowering.

Although the buds seemed to observe my efforts
they didn't open their petals easily.
And even after a week there was no sign of change.

By the time the blossoms of the tulips
and the roses were falling from their stems
the petals of the lilies' budding flowers were only partially open.
Until one day I noticed their gaping mouths and the six petals formed fully.

백합꽃 피우기

아내의 생일선물로 백자에 든
한 다발의 분홍 꽃들을 샀는데
백합 5송이, 튤립 5송이, 장미 5송이는
모두 피어 있었는데 백합 5송이는 아직
피어있지 않았어도
곧 필 거라 생각했다

매일 화병의 물을 갈아주고
줄기 밑 부분을 조금씩 잘라내며
꽃이 피도록 유도했다

그러나 백합 꽃망울은 나의 노력에도 불구하고
일주일이 지나도 아무 변화 없이
좀처럼 피어나지 않았다

튤립 꽃잎이 모두 지고 장미가 모두 줄기에서
떨어질 때까지 백합은 부분적으로만 피더니
어느 날 6개의 꽃잎이 활짝 피어 있는 걸 보았다

Horizontal Line

Nobody can erase the vestige
of the sorrow of parting.

Though it may be embraced
by those who know this pain.

The traces of separation from earth and sky
and between them the evening glow of blood red tears
spread over a horizontal line.

Our meeting was not by chance, but by destiny.
So that we combined into one line horizontally
and our heart, you and I, we are one.

Sunrise and sunset on the line.
We share the pleasure and pain of life together.

지평선

이별의 아픔을 아는 사람들은
그걸 받아들이기도 하겠지만

이별이 주는 슬픔의 흔적을
지울 수 있는 사람은 없다

하늘과 땅을 분리한 흔적
그 하늘과 땅 사이
피눈물 같은 붉은 석양이
지평선에 펼쳐진다

우리의 만남은 우연이 아니고 운명이었다
그래서 우리들은 합쳐 수평으로 하나의 선이 되고
그대와 나의 두 마음도 하나가 된다

일출과 일몰이 한 선에서 일어나듯
우리는 삶의 기쁨과 고통을 함께 하고 있다

Into the Clouds

I entrust my burdensome packages to airport staff.
Submit my weary self to an officer who inspects my body.
And after these bothersome procedures
I fly in an airplane with an empty feeling.

Banks of clouds build up along the western horizon.
We pass small cities just below us.
A river is moving away.
Mountains are receding altogether with long tails.

Like a balloon broken from its string
the plane goes up into the clouds.
I'm shown all kinds of palaces through my window—
villages, houses, animals...

The clouds are like magicians who build the world
without any troublesome measures.
Clouds demonstrate that to live is like the arising of clouds
and dying is like their disappearance.

구름 속으로

무거운 짐은 공항직원에게 맡기고
지친 몸은 검색대 직원에게 맡긴 후
귀찮은 절차가 모두 끝나고 나면
가벼운 마음으로 비행기를 탄다

서쪽 수평선을 따라 구름이 넓게 펼쳐져 있다
비행기 밑으로는 작은 도시들이 지나가고
강이 지나가고 산들이 긴 꼬리를 달고
한꺼번에 지나간다

줄이 끊어진 풍선처럼
비행기가 구름 속으로 들어가니
창문밖에 각양각색의 궁전 마을
집 동물들이 나타난다

구름은 까다로운 절차를 거치지 않고
세상을 창조하는 마술사 같다
구름은 사람이 산다는 것은 구름이
생겨나는 것과 같고 죽는다는 것은 구름이
사라지는 것과 같다는 걸 보여준다

Heavy Rain Showers

After the sweltering heat
that continued for two weeks
rain suddenly pours down.
For more than an hour it continues.

While low clouds hang ominously over the mountains
dark clouds rush in across the horizon.
And then the downtown is filled with deafening thunder—Kaboom!
It grows louder, hour by hour.

A short distance away the towering buildings
grow dim and invisible.
It is dark even in the afternoon.

The cries of birds cease.
They remain at their nesting places
aware of their surroundings.

During storms like these
I also feel the need to cower;
to take a backward glance at what I have been.

소나기

찌는 무더위가 2주 동안 계속되더니
갑자기 비가 퍼붓기 시작해
한 시간 이상 퍼붓는다

음산한 구름이 산에 낮게 깔리고
먹구름이 지평선에서 몰려오자
도심에는 우르르 꽝 하는 천둥소리
시간이 갈수록 천둥소리는 커진다

가까운 고층빌딩이 희미하게 보이더니
이제는 아예 안 보인다
오후시간이지만 어두컴컴하다

새들은 주변 환경을 의식해
울음을 멈추고 둥지를 지킨다

이렇게 폭풍우가 치는 동안에는
나도 칩거하며 지금까지의 삶을
되돌아보는 시간을 가져야하리

To Become One with Rain

First raindrops start to fall with a slow drip-drop...
But this quickly turns into a bigger sound—
pitter-patter, pitter-patter.
Then the flashes of lightning come together
with a mighty bang of thunder.

Crack! Rumble!
Rumble! Crack!
It rains.

Finally, summer showers!
After the hot and muggy weather of the weeks before—
when the air was like the inside of an oven—
it's a welcome relief
when the rain comes down.

Now, lightning flashes
and thunder fills the air.
The sky darkens.

Suddenly, I feel an impulse to run out into the downpour—
to ascend at full speed into the sky.
To become one with the rainstorm completely.

Whenever the thunder rolls, rain streaks the windows heavily.
And at this very moment
light and darkness have exchanged places.

비와 하나 되기

빗방울이 처음에는 천천히 똑똑 떨어지다가
이내 투두둑 하고 큰 소리로 바뀐다
엄청난 굉음의 천둥과 함께 번갯불이 번쩍인다

우르르 꽝!
우르르 꽝!
비가 온다

마침내 여름 소나기다
지난 몇 주 동안 날씨가 뜨겁고 후덥지근해
마치 대기가 끓는 오븐 속 같더니만
이제 비가 내리니 얼마나 다행인가

이제 번갯불이 번쩍거리고
천둥소리가 하늘을 채운다
하늘이 어두워진다

갑자기 나는 쏟아지는 빗속에 뛰어들어
하늘을 향해 전력 질주해
폭풍우와 완전 한 몸이 되고 싶은 충동을 느낀다

천둥이 우르릉거릴 때마다 빗줄기가
창문을 세차게 두드리고
바로 그 순간 빛과 어둠이 교차된다

Story of the Half Moon

In the garden my three-year-old son gestures toward the half moon.
"Where did the other half go?", "Why is it broken?" he asks me.

I remember now that he has seen a full moon only one time.
And I tell him that the other half of the moon is resting somewhere in heaven.

Now, when I look at the half moon, I imagine
the place she rests is somewhere I too could have a relaxing hiatus.

A place where I could restore my soul,
forgetting every inextricably bound thing of this world.

반달 이야기

정원에서 3살짜리 아들이 달을 가리키며
"달 반쪽은 어디로 갔어요?" "떨어져 나갔어요?"
하고 내게 묻는다

그러고 보니 아들은 보름달을 한 번 밖에 보지 못했다
그래서 달 반쪽은
천국 어디쯤에서 쉬고 있을 거라고 말해준다

달을 보고 상상해본다
달 반쪽이 쉬고 있는 곳은
나도 가서 쉴 수 있을 거라고

헤어날 수 없는 세상사 모두 잊고
내 영혼을 회복할 수 있는 곳일 거라고

The Fountain

At a Mediterranean-blue lake in Las Vegas
fountains execute an aquatic ballet
choreographed to music and lights.

Water spouts rise up together, toward space;
swinging right and left with the melody
flexibly forming circles, parabolas, cylindrical bottles.

Some streams play a match—
Shooting upwards continually.
Attempting to reach sky upright.

But in a moment they understand.
There is no support for them on top.
Then they come back home to emptiness.

Sometimes the fountains spray over the air,
creating a misty lake and rainbows.
Night falls, and the colors are illuminated.
Spouts and lights cross over each other with wild abandon.

At midnight the performance stops suddenly.
Music and lights completely covered in darkness.

분수

라스베이거스의 지중해처럼 푸른 호수에는
분수들이 음악과 불빛에 맞춰 수중발레를 한다

물줄기들이 한꺼번에 허공을 향해 솟아올라
음악에 맞춰 좌우로 춤을 추고 원이나 타원
혹은 원통의 병 모양을 부드럽게 만들어 낸다

어떤 물줄기들은 시합이라도 하는 것처럼
하늘까지 닿을 듯 계속 위로 치솟는다

그러나 물줄기들은 꼭대기에 그들을 지탱해 줄
어떤 것도 없다는 걸 금방 알아차리고
제자리의 공허로 되돌아온다

때때로 분수들은 하늘에 물을 뿌려
안개호수와 무지개를 만든다
밤이 오면 색채들은 빛을 발하고
물줄기와 불빛은 어지럽게 교차한다

한밤중에 공연은 갑자기 끝이 나고
음악과 불빛은 어둠속에 파묻힌다

First Birthday

To an infant's bright smiles
we are playing the clown.
Laughing loud and long
at her first birthday party.

The infant keeps on laughing
as we set light to the candles.
We sing birthday songs in celebration
of this first birthday together.

Mortal life and bliss—
She doesn't know, nor does she care,
but creates pretty joy each day.
Opens blossoms, makes flowers.

Merry, merry baby!
What shall we call you?
Happiness and hope we call you.

The green field sleeps in the sun.
The small birds twitter.
The stream is flowing.

Cheerful you are, magnificent you are.
Let us keep your innocent smile long in our heart.
Think of us, lovely baby!

Can we cease to love you
when the candles are extinguished?

No, no! Surely we are with you always.
Until the end of our lives.
We love you forever!

첫돌

아가가 환하게 웃으면
우리는 익살을 부린다
아가의 첫돌잔치에서
한참동안 크게 웃는다

촛불을 켜자 아가는 계속 웃는다
생일축하 노래를 부르며
우리는 아가의 첫돌을 축하한다

언젠가는 소멸될 생명과 지복(至福)--
아가는 모른다 아가는 신경 쓰지도 않는다
그러나 매일 즐거움을 예쁘게 선사해주고
꽃을 피우기도 하고 만들어내기도 한다

명랑한 아가야
너를 무어라 부르면 좋을까
나는 너를 행복과 희망이라 부르리라

햇빛 속에 푸른 들이 잠들어 있다
작은 새들이 지저귄다
시냇물이 흐른다

기쁨의 너, 참 예쁜 너
우리는 네 천진한 미소를 가슴속에 오래 간직하련다
우리 생각을 해다오 사랑스러운 아가야

촛불이 꺼진다고 너에 대한
우리의 사랑이 멈춰질까

아냐 아니야 우리는 우리 삶이
다 할 때까지
너와 함께 할 거야

Retired Men's Picnic

Picnic tables on an autumn afternoon in the village park.
Country friends have gathered for a barbecue cookout.

Each has his role.
One splits the wood for kindling,
another fans the fire; roasting beef on the broiler.
Another carries the meal to the table.

A drinking bout goes on simultaneously.
Some imbibe straight whiskey,
while others drink beer from bottles and cans.

With each drink
their voices grow louder.

They chain smoke.
Revile their old bosses.
Cast aspersions on the president.

One complains about annuity insurance.
Compared to his payment
his pension is too small to live on,
his medical fees too expensive.

They repeat themselves endlessly.
There is no one to hear them.

Only the liquor bottles look up at them
from the corners of their open mouths.

As the afternoon progresses
their tone sinks slowly
into tiredness.

Little by little
the wrinkled faces are buried
in twilight.

은퇴자들의 소풍

가을 오후 마을공원에 놓인 소풍용 식탁
시골친구들이 모여 야외 바비큐파티를 한다

각자가 일을 분담한다
한 사람은 장작용 나무를 패고 한 사람은
불에 부채질을 하고 한 사람은 석쇠에 쇠고기를 굽고
한 사람은 식탁으로 음식을 나른다

술판이 벌어지자 일부는 위스키를 스트레이트로 마시고
일부는 병맥주와 캔 맥주를 마신다

한 잔씩 마실 때 마다
목소리가 커진다

줄담배를 피우고 옛 상관을 욕하고
대통령을 비방한다

한 사람은 연금보험에 대해 불평한다
그가 지급한 보험료에 비해 받는 연금이
너무 작아 살 수가 없고
의료비도 너무 비싸다고 말한다

그들은 같은 말을 끝없이 반복하지만
들어주는 사람은 없다

술병들만이 벌어진 입으로
그들을 쳐다볼 뿐이다.

오후시간이 흘러가자
그들의 말투는 서서히 잦아든다

주름진 얼굴들이
서서히 황혼에 잠겨간다

Renaissance Woman

The Seoul Supermarket is always crowded.
The owner, Mrs. Kim, greets customers with a "Hi."
Shaking hands and all the time smiling a toothy smile.

People prefer to call the market *Hi Super*.

Mrs. Kim is known as a renaissance woman.
Especially knowledgeable about the customs of Asian countries
and daily life in America. Mrs. Kim speaks fluent English.

Her husband, John, also greets every customer with "Hi."
They impart a generosity to Asian, European and African-Americans alike.
They do not forget to create a feast for them.
The customers are like close friends of the Kim's.

Yet, when friends ask to celebrate the Kim's wedding anniversary,
Mrs. Kim doesn't even know the date or the year of the marriage.

르네상스 여인

서울슈퍼마켓은 항상 붐빈다
주인 김여사는 "안녕하세요." 라고 인사를 하며 고객들을
맞이한다
악수를 하며 언제나 이를 다 드러내고 웃는다

사람들은 그 슈퍼마켓을
"하이 슈퍼"라 부른다

김여사는 르네상스여인으로 알려져 있다
아시아 국가들의 관습과 미국인의 일상생활에 특히 정통하다
그녀의 영어는 유창하다

그녀의 남편 존도 모든 고객들을 "안녕하세요." 하며
맞이한다
그 두 사람은 아시아인 유럽인 흑인을 구분하지 않고 똑같이
후하게 대한다
그들의 기념일을 잊지 않고 축하해 준다
고객들은 그들의 친한 친구들이나 다름없다

그러나 친구들이 김여사의 결혼기념일을 축하해주려고 물으면
그녀는 그녀가 결혼한 날이나 연도마저 모른다

65

Dimple

Mary was my neighbor twenty years ago,
then left for New York City.
After that I forgot her.

By chance I met her at the shopping mall.
But when she called to me I didn't recognize her.
Her face was that of a common middle-aged lady.

At first I didn't answer.

Then she called me again, "Brother!
You are the same, like a young man."
And a smile spread across her face.

Then unexpectedly,
another Mary came out
from behind the aged lady's face.
Then I remembered her dimples when she smiled.

Her two high school daughters, taller than she
broke into a chorus of dimpled laughter.
Which, until this time, they had kept,
like a flower, all to themselves.

보조개

메리는 20년 전 내 이웃이었는데
뉴욕시로 이사를 간 후에는 그녀를 잊고 살았다

그러다 우연히 쇼핑몰에서 만난 그녀가
내 이름을 불렀으나 흔한 중년여인의 얼굴을 한
그녀를 내가 알아보지 못했다

그래서 처음에는 대답을 못했다

그러자 그녀가 "오빠" 하고 다시 부르며
"오빠는 예전 젊었을 때와 똑 같군요" 라고 말하는 순간
그녀의 얼굴에 번지는 미소를 보았다

그때 예상 밖에도 나이 먹은 여인의 얼굴 뒤에서
또 한 사람의 메리가 나타났다 그때서야 나는 그녀가
웃을 때 생기는 보조개를 기억해 냈다

그녀보다 키가 더 큰 고등학생 두 딸이
그들만의 전매특허로 여태 간직해온 꽃 같은
보조개 웃음을 동시에 터뜨리고 있었다

I Am Flying

I am flying in a plane over the Pacific; it is midnight.
I sleep in a lounge chair facing upward.
My first time flying business class.
The seat is as comfortable as the billowing clouds outside the window.

Up until now I sat in the narrow seats of economy class
unable to recline fully.
The front of the plane, first class,
is a place I had never experienced.

Before I had no interest in the classes of a plane.
Going by air was enough for me;
I never thought of comparing classes.
The idea of sitting in business class was someone else's story.
And I didn't care about other people's comfortable circumstances.

There are so many passengers in the back rows of the plane.
Before, I didn't feel the inconvenience of the constricted seats.
I feel compassion for them now,
as they sleep
curled up in their narrow seats.

We are all passengers in the same outer space.
Located at around thirty thousand feet.
Our departure time and destination the same.
Flying time will be around eleven hours,
but we are segregated by classes of seats.

Before, I could perceive the comfort of business class.
But when I imagined the first class seats
my business class seat also seemed insufficient.
In order to enjoy the comfortable life, perhaps,
we must look back into the past life of poverty.

비행기 안에서

나는 비행기를 타고 태평양 위를 날고 있다
한밤중이다
나는 천장을 향한 안락의자에서 잠을 잔다
비즈니스 클래스를 타는 건 처음이다
좌석이 비행기 창밖에 피어난 구름처럼 편하다

지금까지 나는 이코노미 클래스로 여행을 했기 때문에
좌석에 충분히 몸을 눕힐 수 없었다
비행기 앞 일등석은 한 번도 타본 적이 없다

전에는 비행기 좌석등급에 전혀 관심이 없었다
비행기를 타는 것만으로 만족했다
비즈니스클래스는 다른 사람의 이야기였다
게다가 나는 다른 사람들이 편하게 여행하는 것에는
관심이 없었다

비행기 뒷좌석에 많은 사람들이 앉아있다
전에는 협소한 좌석으로 인해 불편함을 못 느꼈다
그러나 나는 지금 좁은 좌석에 몸을 웅크리고
잠을 자는 사람들에게 연민을 느낀다

우리는 모두 약 3만 피트 고도와 같은 우주공간에
있는 승객들이다
우리의 출발시간과 도착시간도 같다
비행시간은 11시간정도지만 우리는 서로 다른 등급의
좌석에 의해 분리돼 있다

전에는 비즈니스클래스가 편하다는 걸 알고는 있었으나
일등석을 머릿속에 떠올리니 비즈니스클래스도 충분치
않다는 생각을 하게 된다
지금 편히 잘 살고 있다는 걸 깨달으려면 가난하게
살았던 옛 시절을 되돌아 봐야할 것 같구나

At the Adult School

Isabella, a working mom with two jobs,
repeats the words in English
she is trying to memorize.

Before her eyes they seem to escape.
As soon as a word enters her right ear
it vanishes from her left.

Before she completes a page in her textbook
she forgets the contents of the first line.
Her second daughter's crying face appears in her memory.
The daughter who has caught a cold, again.

Isabella works at the laundry, part-time weekday afternoons;
at a fine restaurant in the evenings.
But she is dreaming of becoming a police officer.

Her classmate Daniel is an auto mechanic.
He is looking for words
in the dictionary
while listening to the teacher's lecture.

An old man who is retired writes words on a page.
He'd like to write his memoir in English.

Fifty students, whose motherland and races are different,
share their enthusiasm for revealing that their difficulties are the same.

성인학교

두 가지 직업을 가진 워킹맘 이사벨라는
암기해야 하는 말들을 영어로 반복해 본다

그러나 그것들이 눈앞에서 사라져 버리는 것 같다
한 귀로 들어오는 순간 다른 귀로 나가 버린다

교과서 한 페이지를 마치기 전에 첫 줄의 내용을
잊어버린다
그녀의 감기 걸린 둘째딸의 우는 얼굴이 자꾸만 떠오른다

이사벨라는 주중 오후시간에는 세탁소에서
파트 타임으로 일하고 저녁시간에는 고급식당에서
일하지만 경찰이 되는 꿈을 갖고 있다

그녀의 급우 다니엘은 자동차 정비공인데 선생님의
강의를 들으면서 사전에서 단어를 찾고 있다

은퇴한 노인이 종이에 영어단어를 적고 있다
그는 자신의 회고록을 영어로 쓰고 싶어 한다

나라와 인종이 다른 50명의 학생들이 모두
하나같이 동일한 어려움을 겪고 있다는 것을
열정적으로 보여주고 있다

Dozing

I wake to the sound of a waterfall—
a cruise over invisible Buffalo Falls;
I hear a burst of applause.

I notice a pool of saliva on my tan jacket;
Wipe it up.
Try not to doze off again.

To chase off my drowsiness
I hit my thigh, clear my throat, rub my eyes;
Certainly not! I will not fall asleep again!

I admonish myself.
Tilt my head to concentrate.
Absorb the lecture on philosophy.

After awhile I wake
to the noise of a crashing waterfall again.
But there is no water.

Only the din of applause
in the full conference room.

I ask myself: *Isn't this strange?*
I've never napped before
while listening to a teacher's lecture.

In this somnolent condition
I see myself now, trying to awaken.
But all self-persuasion is in vain.

As soon as I let myself off the hook
I plunge into Buffalo Falls again.
Startled by laughter as I shout for help.

졸음

나는 폭포소리에 잠을 깬다
눈에 안 보이는 버펄로 폭포 유람선 여행이다
박수가 터져 나오는 소리가 들린다

나는 황갈색 상의에 흘린 침을 보고 닦아낸다
다시는 잠들지 않으려 애를 쓴다

졸음을 쫓으려 허벅지를 때리고 목을 가다듬고 눈을 비빈다
"절대 졸면 안 돼. 다시는 잠들지 않을 거야!"

나는 고개를 한쪽으로 기울이고 집중해라
철학 강의를 들어라 하고 스스로를 타이른다

잠시 후 나는 폭포가 떨어지는
굉음에 잠을 깬다

그러나 사람이 가득 들어찬 회의실에 소음만 있을 뿐
물은 한 방울도 보이지 않는다

나는 자문해 본다 "이것 좀 이상하지 않아?
선생님 강의 중에 나는 한 번도 낮잠을 잔 적이
없는데..."

이렇게 졸린 상태가 되어 나는 깨어나려고 애를 쓴다
그러나 아무리 내 자신을 설득해 봐도 소용이 없다

나 자신을 내려놓는 순간 나는
다시 버펄로 폭포 속으로 떨어진다
내가 구조해 달라 외칠 때
웃음이 터져 나오고 나는 깜짝 놀란다

Mountain in the Foreground

The mountain in the foreground of my village forecasts the weather.
In the morning I see the mountain's features from my bed.
Sunny days are a short distance away.

Sometimes dark clouds move across the mountain,
linger for a while on the ridge, then disappear
suddenly.

On other days gigantic cumulus clouds
hang on its peak—
a huge balloon.

In rainy season the mountain is covered with clouds,
the mountain invisible for days.
Heavy clouds rush across the ridgeline,
then showers follow.

Sometimes the fog covers the forest,
spreads her skirt
all the way to the village.

In the evening the sky over the mountain
shows a halo 'round the moon.
And then I forecast it will rain tomorrow.

The mountain changes his clothes every season.
Sometimes it is green;
After that the hills are aflame with autumnal hues.
Even when I do not notice.

The mountain ridge is the gate of the sun, the moon and the birds.
Flocks of swans fly away just before sunset—
Orange in a sky full of purple feathers.
Before the winter snowcaps appear on top of the hill.

마을 앞산

내가 사는 마을 앞산은 일기예보를 한다
아침에 나는 침대에서 산의 모습을 보고
화창한 날이 될 것임을 안다

때때로 먹구름이 산을 통과하던 중
산마루에 잠시 머물다 갑자기 사라진다

어떤 날에는 거대한 뭉게구름이
산의 정상에 걸려있다

우기에는 산은 구름에 가려 수일동안 산을 볼 수가 없다
짙은 구름이 산의 능선을 따라 몰려오면
소나기가 쏟아진다

때로는 안개가 숲을 덮고
산 전체를 가린 후 마을까지 넘어온다

저녁에 산 위의 하늘에 떠오른 달 주변에
광륜이 생겨나면 내일 비가 올 것임을
예측할 수 있다

산은 계절마다 새 옷으로 갈아입는다
내가 주목하고 있지 않아도 한 때 초록이었던
산은 나중에는 가을빛으로 불탄다

산마루는 태양과 달과 새들을 찾아가는 관문이다
일몰 직전 자주 빛 깃털로 가득 찬 오렌지색
하늘로 백조 떼가 날아간다
산 정상이 흰 눈으로 덮이는
겨울이 오기 전에 살 곳을 찾아서

II.

Highway 5

I am driving from San Diego to San Francisco.
It is midnight.
In the rearview mirror of my minivan,
trucks, wagons and sedans pass me.

A limousine with opened windows
pulls up beside me.
The driver yawns heavily.
In a pink sleeveless dress a woman leans
on the arm of a man driving a convertible.

My speedometer reads seventy-five miles an hour.
I've already gulped three glasses of iced coffee,
but still feel drowsy.
Turned up the MP3 player.
Sung a song loudly.

I stretch my lower jaw right and left with a yawn.
The GPS reveals
the distance and time
left to travel.
I pinch the flesh of my thigh.
But it is all the same, sleepy.

In a few hours I will arrive home.
If I get over this moment.
But it is not easy.

This trip is hard like the stern realities of my life.
Troubles must be passed through.
Nobody can drive my life for me.
I will plow my way along the road.

If I get over this moment
the darkness will certainly be over.
The sun will shine brilliantly.

My heart is in my home, not here on the highway.
My heart lives for the coming day.
When there is an end to passing troubles.
And delight returns.

고속도로 5

나는 운전을 해 샌디에이고에서 샌프란시스코로 가고 있다
한밤중이다
내가 운전하는 미니밴의 백미러를 통해 트럭과 왜건과
세단이 나를 스쳐 지나가는 걸 본다

창문이 열린 리무진 한 대가 내 곁으로 다가온다
운전자는 크게 하품을 한다
소매 없는 핑크색 드레스를 입은 여인이 오픈카를 운전하는
남자의 팔에 기대어 있다

속도계를 보니 시속 75마일이다
얼음을 넣은 커피를 벌써 석 잔이나 마셨지만 졸린다
MP3 볼륨을 올리고 노래를 크게 부른다

하품을 하면서 아래턱을 좌우로 움직여 본다
GPS가 아직 남은 거리와 시간을 보여준다
나는 허벅지살을 꼬집는다 그래도 졸리기는 마찬가지다

몇 시간 후면 나는 집에 도착하리라
이 순간만 잘 극복한다면
그러나 그게 쉽지가 않다

이 여행은 가혹한 나의 현실만큼이나 힘들다
나는 이 고난들을 헤쳐 나가야한다
아무도 나 대신에 내 삶을 살아주지 않는다
나는 나의 길을 따라 밭을 갈 것이다

내가 이 순간을 이겨낸다면
어둠도 반드시 끝날 것이다
밝은 태양이 비출 것이다

내 마음은 여기 고속도로에 있는 게 아니고 집에 가 있다
내 마음은 다가오는 날에 가 있다
고난이 모두 지나가면 기쁜 날이 다시 찾아온다

Surfing

I am surfing today, in the middle of the boundless Pacific.
Surfing on the rough waves.
Though I am exposed to rain and wind everyday
I continue surfing.

Even if great waves the size of mountains arise,
I will not stop,
nor stumble,
but only manage them to move forward.

Sometimes the waves are calm.
But at any time without notice
a huge wave tackles me,
causes me to keel over
into deep water.

Waves are my close friends,
neighbors, my life's companions;
I cannot live without them.

Sea conditions may vary from time to time,
but in order to survive life's harsh passages
I choose waves that aren't too big or too little.

I am surfing today.
I am going through the rough waves
alone.

서핑

나는 오늘 끝없이 넓은 태평양 한가운데서
서핑을 하고 있다 거친 파도를 타고 넘는 서핑
비와 바람 속에서도 나는 서핑을 계속한다

산더미 같은 파도가 몰려와도
나는 멈추지도 않고 넘어지지도
않으면서 파도를 타고 앞으로 나아간다

파도가 잠잠할 때도 있다
그러나 언제라도 예고 없이 거대한 파도가 나를 덮쳐
깊은 물속으로 밀어 넣는다

파도는 나의 친한 친구요 이웃이요
내 인생의 동반자다
파도 없이는 혼자 살 수 없다

바다상태는 수시로 변한다
삶의 힘든 고비에서 살아남기 위해 나는 너무 크거나
너무 작지 않은 파도를 선택한다

나는 오늘도 서핑을 한다
거친 파도를 혼자 넘는다

Leave It as It Is

I see her from across the channel liner,
a nameless, uninhabited, lush island
at the bosom of the Pacific
between San Francisco and Los Angeles.

Like an inquisitive child
she is on intimate terms with nature.

The birds begin to sing before the sun rises.
Those echoes resound
and the crystal streams glide
through the valley.

Buds come into bloom.
The merry birds sing a joyous song
while the young lambs bound
under leaves so green.

What beautiful scenery there is!

Breezes pass through the leaves.
She wants to sleep by the murmuring stream.
Disturb not her dream.

Pass through her land without stopping.
Flow gently to the seashore.
Don't drop your anchor to come up.
Don't pitch a tent, don't dig a well.
Flow gently along with the shore.

Her heart leaps up when she sees
a rainbow in the sky.
She is singing a song, the winds are breathing low
and the stars are burning bright.

Flow gently by, disturb not her land.
Leave her as she is.
Leave it as it is.

내버려 두라

나는 연락선을 타고 가다 샌프란시스코와
로스앤젤레스 사이 태평양 끝자락에 사람도 살지 않고
이름도 없는 숲이 울창한 섬 하나를 발견한다

섬은 호기심 많은 아이처럼
자연과 잘 어울린다

새가 해 뜨기 전에 노래를 시작하자
새 노래 소리가 메아리 치고
수정 같이 맑은 물이 계곡사이로 흐른다

섬에는 꽃이 핀다
흥겨운 새들이 즐겁게 노래하고 여러 마리의 새끼 양들이
푸른 나무아래서 풀을 뜯고 있다

이 얼마나 아름다운 풍경인가

미풍이 나뭇잎사이로 지나간다
섬은 졸졸 흐르는 시냇물 소리에 잠이 든다
섬이 꾸는 꿈을 방해하지 말라

멈추지 말고 섬을 그냥 통과하라
해안까지 부드럽게 흘러가라
섬에 오르려고 닻을 내리지 말라
텐트도 치지 말고 우물도 파지 말라
그냥 해안을 따라 부드럽게 흘러가라

섬은 하늘의 무지개를 보고 가슴을 두근거린다
섬이 노래를 하고 바람은 나지막하게 숨을 쉬고
별이 밝게 빛난다

섬을 부드럽게 지나가되 방해하지 말라
섬을 있는 그대로 내버려 두라
있는 그대로 내버려 두라

New York City

The city of all cities!
The city where people from every country live together.

At the United Nations' headquarters
you will be welcomed by the flags of all nations
flapping in the sparkling sunshine.
The flag of your homeland inspiring proud memories.

All the busy people!
Even so, when we struggle to find our way,
they help us kindly.
They do not lose their laughter.

When the stress of daily life accumulates
they go to Times Square
to sing and dance with friends.
Or take a break alone in midtown's Central Park.

When frustrating days greet you
look to the Statue of Liberty—icon of freedom.
She might give you wings
to fly to endless blue sky.

Thus and so, a beautiful night descends.
Numberless stars alight over the city.
Each room in the high-rise apartments is full of stories.
New Yorkers everywhere, like lovers that talk all night,
and awaken to conceive a happy dream the next morning.

뉴욕시

도시 중의 도시
모든 나라에서 온 사람들이 함께 사는 도시

유엔본부에 가면 반짝이는 햇살 속에 펄럭이는
세계 모든 나라들의 깃발이 방문객을 반갑게 맞아준다
자랑스러운 추억을 생각나게 하는 그대 조국의 깃발

모두가 다 바쁜 사람들
그러나 우리가 길을 힘들게 찾는 걸 보면
웃음을 잃지 않고 친절하게 안내를 해준다

일상의 스트레스가 쌓이면 그들은 타임스 스퀘어에 가서
친구들과 노래를 부르고 춤을 추거나
시내 한가운데 있는 센트럴파크에 가서 홀로 휴식을 취한다

좌절감을 느끼는 날에는 자유의 상징인 자유의
여신상을 바라보라 여신이 그대에게 끝없이 푸른 하늘로
날아갈 날개를 달아줄지도 모르니

이윽고 아름다운 밤이 되면 도시로 무수한 별들이 빛나고
고층아파트 각 방에서는 이야기 꽃이 피어난다
어디를 가든 뉴욕 시민들은 연인들처럼 밤새 대화를 하고
다음날 아침이면 행복한 꿈에서 깨어난다

The Umbrella

Autumn in New York's Central Park.
Rain again.

The fallen leaves once yellow, now brownish in color.
Scattered by the steps of visitors.

Autumn rains press the leaves to fall.

An old man sees a young couple
walking in front of him
under a partially torn
black umbrella.

The young man
holds the umbrella with one hand.
With the other
he hugs the young woman at her waist.

Her arms entwined around his.
They are completely together.

Even though they are under the umbrella
they are soaked by the rain:
their shoulders, trousers, shoes.
Even though, they walk along humming.
Sometimes bursting into laughter.

The harder it rains
the closer they hug.
The umbrella binds them together.
A small and torn umbrella is joy enough.

우산

뉴욕 센트럴 파크의 가을
비가 또 내린다

노란색 낙엽들은 이제 연한 갈색으로 변했다
공원을 찾은 사람들 발길에 부딪혀 흩어진다

가을비에 낙엽이 진다

찢어진 까만 우산을 쓰고 앞서 걸어가는 젊은 남녀를
노인 한 사람이 바라본다

젊은 남자는 한 손으로 우산을 잡고 다른 손으로는
젊은 여자의 허리를 안고 있다

여자의 팔은 남자의 팔을 감고 있다
두 사람은 완전히 하나다

남녀는 우산을 쓰고는 있지만 어깨 바지
신발 할 것 없이 모두 비에 흠뻑 젖어 있다
걸어가며 콧노래를 부르고 때로는 웃음을 터뜨린다

비가 세차질수록 그들은 더욱 서로를 껴안는다
우산이 그들을 한데로 묶어주고 있다
작고 찢어진 우산만으로도 그들은 즐겁다

Some Salesmen

David returns to Wall Street
where he and Michel sold
clothes and shoes.

They were poor and happy together then.
Driving their old Volkswagen Bus,
selling goods at a loss and at clearance.

Sometimes in the evenings they drank beer.
Disputed capitalism and business etiquette
all night long.

Once they opened a very small store
on the corner
of a back street.

Though they did their best
day and night to survive, t
hey finally closed it down.

Left with debt,
they scattered
each on their own.

The survival game too cold.

Now David stands in front of the banks at noon.
The buildings more magnificent and splendid than before.
There are many bankers in formal attire;
their faces beaming with smiles.

The small stores on the back streets are still shabby.
Many confusing signs have appeared,
but few people to read them.
Salesmen solicit them with no concern.

On the other side of the main street
hundreds of people are marching.
Demonstrating with the placard "Occupy Wall Street."
Shouting the slogan "We are the ninety-nine percent!" over and over.

But their slogan only scatters into the air.

어떤 세일즈맨

데이비드는 마이클과 함께 옷과 신발을 팔던
월 스트리트로 돌아간다

함께 장사를 할 때 두 사람은 가난했지만 행복했다
낡은 폭스바겐 버스로 물건을 밀지고 팔거나
재고정리 가격으로 팔았다

때로는 저녁에 맥주를 마시고 밤새도록 자본주의와
비즈니스 에티켓에 관해 논쟁을 했다

뒷골목 한구석에 아주 작은
가게를 열기도 했다

그들은 살아남기 위해 밤낮으로 최선을 다 했지만
결국에는 문을 닫을 수밖에 없었다

빚만 지고 그들은
각자 제 갈 길을 갔다

생존게임은 너무나 매서웠다

지금 데이비드는 정오에 은행 문 앞에 서 있다
은행건물은 전보다 더 멋지고 아름답다
정장을 한 많은 은행원들은 환하게 웃고 있다

뒷골목의 작은 가게들은 아직도 초라하기만 하다
어지러운 간판들이 많이 생겨났지만 간판을 보는 사람은
거의 없다
세일즈맨들은 건성으로 호객행위를 한다

큰 길 다른 쪽에는 수백 명의 사람들이 행진을 하고 있다
"월가를 점령하라" 라는 플래카드를 들고 데모를 한다
"우리는 99%다" 라는 슬로건을 반복해서 외치고 있다

그러나 그들의 슬로건은
허공으로 사라질 뿐이다

Statue of Liberty

Legendary heroine, our pride.
Prophetess who wakes up the people. Guardian deity of America.

In silence she asks those who are weary and oppressed to follow.
To look at the torchlight in her right hand,
hold a dream for the future,
keep on moving toward tomorrow.

Her exclamation echoes in our hearts and minds:
Through the Freedom Tower, New York,
over oceans, throughout the world.

She is a mute pioneer.
There are no words that come from her.
But her grand silent gesture
is more eloquent than speech.

자유의 여신상

전설의 여주인공 우리의 긍지
사람들을 일깨우는 예언자
미국의 수호신

침묵 속에서 그녀는 지치고 억압받는 자들에게
그녀의 오른 손에 들린 횃불을 바라보고
미래에 대한 꿈을 갖고 내일을 향해
전진하라고 권유하고 있다

그녀의 외침은 우리의 가슴과
마음속에 메아리 친 후
뉴욕의 자유의 탑을 지나
대서양을 지나 전 세계로 울려 퍼지고 있다

그녀는 침묵의 선구자이기에
그녀가 내 뱉는 말은 없다
그녀의 장엄한 침묵의 몸짓은
말보다 더 웅변적이다

Ground Zero Memorial

In the memorial pools
the gentle melody of waves
softly resounding.

Victims' names etched on the surrounding panels
seem to go down with the waves.
Hand in hand in a gentle rhythm.

Waves cascade into a hole in the middle
together with noise and dust
hatred and earthly thoughts…

While the black hole before us in the center of the pool
absorbs all things—even the light—
the waves continue and continue.

It seems that through the waves
all things in nature are refined
and settle into another harmonic universe.

Perhaps visitors understand—like pilgrims to other sacred places—
that what is seen is temporary, what is unseen is eternal.
That to love is to keep an eon of silence hanging over them.

그라운드 제로 기념비

메모리얼 풀안에
잔잔한 멜로디가 울려 퍼진다

벽에 새겨진 희생자 이름들이
손에 손을 잡고 물결처럼 내려가며 속삭인다

새소리 소음과 먼지
미움과 사연들을 안고 중앙의 풀속으로
흘러들어간다

중앙의 블랙홀에서
빛을 포함한 모든 것을 받아들인다

물결의 흐름 속에
삼라만상이 정제되고 변화되어
다른 세상으로 안치되는 듯

방문객들도 다른 성지의 순례자들처럼
삶과 사후를 이해하는 듯
보이는 것은 순간이요
보이지 않는 것이 영원하다는 것을
그리고 사랑은 영원히 침묵하는 거라는 것을

A Writing Class by the Railroad

Our classroom resembles a rural hut in the countryside,
in a renovated railroad station on the Hudson Valley.
The seasons seem to arrive earlier here.

At the writers' center students cultivate their creativity.
Exchanging opinions like farmers in this valley—
trading seeds, talking over the weather.
Their discussions continue until evening.

The sound of the railroad sparks their imagination.
The whistle so loud they cannot speak, but only look to each other.
Their hopes spreading out further, following the endless railroad.
Propelling them to fly upward toward blue skies, like the birds of this valley.

At the writing class on the Hudson River where the yachts anchor,
students primp their feathers like showy canvases to sail.
They are a step ahead of the seasons,
their enthusiasm leading the way.

Despite the noise of the train
the roses bloom beautifully
and the red apples are ripe on the trees.

기차 길 옆 창작 교실

보수공사를 마친 허드슨 밸리의 낡은 기차역
글쓰기 교실은 계절이 다른 곳보다 먼저 찾아오는
시골 오두막집을 닮았다

글쓰기 교실에는 수십 명의 학생들이 시골 마을
농부들이 씨를 거래하고 날씨를 이야기하듯
서로 의견을 교환하며 그들의 창작력을 키운다
그들의 토론은 저녁까지 계속된다

시끄러운 기차 소리는 그들의 상상력을 자극한다
시끄러워 말을 못 할 때면 그들은 서로를 바라본다
그들의 희망은 끝없는 철길을 따라 멀리 펼쳐지고
그들로 하여금 새처럼 푸른 하늘로 날아오르게 한다

요트가 정박하는 허드슨 강에 위치한 글쓰기 교실에는
학생들이 항해에 필요한 돛을 정비하고
새가 깃털을 가다듬는 것 같은 준비를 한다
그들은 계절보다 한발 앞서갈 뿐만 아니라
그들이 하는 일에 대해서도 커다란 열정을 가지고 있다

시끄러운 소리 속에서도 장미는 아름답게 피고
사과는 빨갛게 익는다

Outside the National Cemetery

White magnolias brightly bloom
in the isolated places outside the national cemetery.

The white gravestones lined up in the cemetery
welcome the magnolias that come each year in April.

Wearing their white uniforms, the magnolias are like officers in the navy
receiving an inspection from their admiral.

The captivated white petals console the souls in the cemetery.
The souls of those who laid down their lives for their nation.

The souls beneath the gravestones have eagerly waited a long time
for their friends and relatives.

The magnolias ghostwrite the letters for the souls in their petals
and send them on the breeze to those who live in remote parts of the country.

On windy days they sing the song of April and dance with the branches
scattering the petals on the graves.

In the night sky interspersed with stars
the souls and petals are dreaming a dream together.

국립묘지 밖

국립묘지 밖 외딴곳에
하얀 목련꽃이 활짝 피었다

묘지 안에 늘어선 묘비들이
매년 4월에 피는 목련꽃을 반긴다

목련꽃들은 하얀 제복을 입고
제독의 검열을 받는 해군 장병들 같다

매혹적인 하얀 꽃잎들은 나라를 위해 목숨을 바친 후
묘지에 누워있는 영혼들을 위로해 준다

묘석 밑에 누운 영혼들은 오랫동안
친구나 친척들이 찾아 주기를 갈망해 왔다

목련은 자신의 꽃잎들에다 영혼들의 편지를 대필한 다음
미풍에 실어 멀리 있는 그들에게 보내준다

바람 부는 날이면 목련은 나뭇가지들과 함께
4월의 노래를 부르고 춤을 추며 꽃잎을 무덤에 뿌린다

영혼들과 꽃잎들은 별이 빛나는
밤하늘에서 함께 꿈을 꾼다

At the Unknown Soldiers' Monument

An invisible banner.
Unheard cry.
Of legendary heroes.
Obscure names.

We forgot you like a lost memory.
Enjoyed life with drinking and song
until hearing a trumpeter's requiem
on Memorial Day...

We look at the bundled flowers
before the spirits of the departed.
We pray and confess our stupidity.

You sink into oblivion while we consume ourselves.
Flinging our bodies into the sea of humanity,
in a fierce struggle for existence.

Your monuments are rusted with unfulfilled desires.
What shall we say to those
who know righteousness?

Where is the chorus of the people?
You know those who stand proudly by the flag.
You were not born for fading away.

Phoenixes!
If there is a true patriot
you are one!

Generations forget you and we are selfish.
But you are our lost conscience.
Keeper of morality until the end of time.

무명용사 기념탑에서

보이지 않는 깃발
소리 없는 외침
전설적 영웅들
알려지지 않은 이름들

우리는 추억을 잊듯 그대들을 잊었습니다
트럼펫 연주로 진혼곡을 들을 때까지
마시고 노래하며 인생을 즐겼습니다

영령들 앞에 놓인 꽃다발을 보고서야
기도를 올리며 우리의 어리석음을 고백합니다

우리가 무서운 생존경쟁에서 살아남기 위해
우리 몸을 세상의 바다에 던져
우리 자신을 소모시키는 동안
그대들은 잊혀지고 있습니다

그대들을 위한 기념비는
이루지 못한 욕망으로 녹슬어 있습니다
정의를 아는 사람들에게 우리는 뭐라고 말할까요

사람들이 함께 부르는 합창은 어디에 있나요
자랑스럽게 깃발을 지키는 사람들을
그대들은 알고 있습니다.
그대들은 잊혀지려고 세상에 태어나지 않았습니다

불사조!
애국자가 있다면 그대들이 애국자입니다

여러 세대가 그대들을 잊어왔고
우리는 이기적 존재들이었습니다
그러나 그대들은 우리의 잃어버린 양심이요
영원한 도덕의 수호자들입니다

By the Hudson River

In the lonely autumn evening I sit by the Hudson River
and watch a passing train.
After awhile a whistle sounds along the curving pathway.

In the distance the George Washington Bridge is decorated
with sparkling headlights from the vehicles
that are lined up bumper-to-bumper on the road.

The river currents heave and set.
I see a shooting star for a fleeting moment.

How many evenings have I sat alone on this bank,
watching the river's panorama!
If there were no whistles here or headlights or stars,
what a desolate place before me.

But the river flows, trains run, and
meteors fall. I too drift and surge.
Sending my yearning for my home country, to and fro.

허드슨 강변에서

외로운 가을저녁 허드슨 강변에 앉아
지나가는 기차를 바라본다
기차는 구부러진 길을 따라 기적을 울린다

길게 늘어선 자동차들의 전조등이
멀리 조지워싱턴교를 화려하게 장식한다

강물이 출렁인다
순식간에 유성 한 개가 떨어진다

이 강변에 나 홀로 앉아 강을 바라보며
얼마나 많은 저녁시간을 보냈던가
이곳에 기적소리나 전조등이나 별이 없다면
얼마나 황량하게 느껴질까

강은 흐르고 기차는 달리고 유성은 떨어지고
나 또한 고향을 그리워하며 이리저리 떠돌고 있다

The Train Whistle

Because New Jersey's Harrington Park is awakened from its deep slumber
early mornings by the train whistle
there is no need to set an alarm for rising.

The train's shriek causes a stampede of livestock and birds
and other creatures emerge from the forest.
Then the sparrows, hares, and deer are awakened.

Though it is noisy, sometimes this distant shrill sound
creates a longing in me for my home country.

Where poor inhabitants, with no watches to guide them,
welcome the useful whistle—
Informing them what time to have lunch at a farm field far away,
when to dwell and leave again.

The trains pass through the forest and the villages
every day,
in all seasons.

The whistle blows:
Choo-choo, Choo-choo,
Toot-toot, Toot-toot...

기적

뉴저지 해밀턴 공원은
이른 아침 기적소리에 깨어난다
아침 기상을 위해 자명종을 맞출 필요가 없다

기적 소리에 참새 토끼 사슴을 포함한
모든 동물들이 일시에 깨어난다
동물과 새들이 기적소리를 듣고 숲에서 움직이기 시작한다

시끄럽기는 하지만 먼 기적소리는 때때로
나의 조국에 대한 그리움을 불러일으킨다

그곳의 가난한 주민들은 시계가 없기 때문에
멀리 떨어진 논과 밭에서 언제 점심을 먹고
언제까지 일을 하다 언제 귀가해야 하는지를 알려주는
쓸모 많은 기적소리를 반겼다

기차는 사시사철 하루도 빠지지 않고
숲과 마을을 지나간다

삑－삑－삑
뚜－뚜－뚜

Nightmare

When I sit on the bank of the Hudson River,
it blows a squall
and the river is roaring and tumultuous.

Two large dragons with long horns come out of the water,
very ugly and lean, fiercely fighting with each other,
their mouths fully open.

And as I look more closely
two small frogs, fat and sleek
are seated on the horns of each dragon.

When the monsters shrink to the size and shape of a bean
the frogs swallow them whole.
First the sleek one, then the fat one.

Now a shiny frog sits on my upper eyelids and cries all night long,
frequently crossing from my right eye to my left.
Suddenly the frog is dressed in spots of white and green.

Each time he cries, a white balloon, bigger than his entire body
inflates and deflates in his mouth.
As its red tongue repeatedly darts in and out.

Suddenly he slurps my body down inside his mouth!
I utter a full-throated shriek at the frightening sound,
as my wife wakes me with an equally shrill loudness.

악몽

허드슨 강변에 앉아있으니
돌풍이 불어와 강물에 큰 소요가 일어난다

흉측하고 여윈 두 마리 용이 강물에서 나와
입을 크게 벌리고 서로 무섭게 싸운다

더 자세히 보니 통통한 개구리와 날씬한 개구리가
두 마리 용의 뿔을 하나씩 차지하고 앉아있다

용들의 몸집이 콩 같은 크기와 모습으로 줄어들자
개구리들이 그것들을 통째로 삼켜버리는데
날씬한 개구리가 먼저 삼키고
통통한 개구리가 다음에 삼킨다

그러자 빛이 나는 개구리가 내 눈꺼풀 위에 앉아 있다가
자꾸만 나의 오른쪽 눈에서 왼쪽 눈으로 건너간다
갑자기 개구리 몸에 흰색과 초록색 반점이 생겨난다

개구리가 울 때마다 풍선이 개구리 몸보다 더 크게
부풀어 올랐다가 혀를 계속 널름거리는
개구리의 입속으로 들어가 오므라든다

갑자기 개구리가 내 몸을 후루룩 삼켜버린다
개구리가 나를 삼키는 소리에 놀라
나는 목이 터져라 비명을 지르고
내 비명소리에 놀란 아내가
똑 같이 비명을 질러 나를 깨운다

A Place Where Clouds Are Flowing

On a grassy knoll by the Hudson River, I lie down with my head on my arms.
To the west many clouds are floating about
at the mercy of the wind.

An airplane is flying high through the clouds; my eyes follow it.
My yearning is wafted on the breeze
and chases the clouds.

I long to fly far off
where clouds go.

The clouds that seem to beckon with hands,
the clouds I wish to follow.

Hoping to visit a beatific place
like a childhood dream.

My imaginings take me to a land
over the continent, across the ocean.

To my beloved homeland
where I first fell in love.

So over the clouds
like a flower that blossoms
I send my love.

구름이 흘러가는 곳

허드슨 강변 잔디밭에
팔베개를 하고 누워있으니
구름 떼가 바람 따라 서편으로 흘러간다

비행기 한 대가 구름을 뚫고 날아오르자
나의 시선은 비행기를 따라가고

내 가슴속 그리움은
구름을 따라간다

나는 구름이 가는 곳까지
날아 가보고 싶다

내게 손짓하는 듯한 구름
내가 따라가 보고 싶은 구름

유년의 꿈처럼 기쁨이 넘치는 곳으로
가보고 싶다

대륙을 지나 바다를 건너
사랑에 빠졌던 내가 가장 사랑하는
나의 고국으로 가는 것을 상상해보고

꽃같이 피어나는 구름너머로
내 사랑을 보낸다

In a Blacksmith Shop

The dragon tattoos on the solid muscles of both forearms come alive
as the blacksmith shapes a sharp knife on the anvil.

With the might of his strong arms
he manages skillfully with one hand holding a tong,
the other a hammer, as steel yields.

At first when steel enters the blacksmith shop it is cold and stiff.
But on the anvil even stubborn and wild steel has no choice
but to succumb.

After getting red in the face,
from the heat of the flames and the thrust of the hammer,
the steel becomes a milder character.

At one time, both anvil and hammer were wild steel.
But now they are producing useful things
together with their master.

대장간에서

대장장이가 예리한 칼을 모루에서 만드니
그의 양 팔뚝의 단단한 근육에 새겨진
용의 문신이 되살아난다

강한 팔 힘으로 그는 능숙하게 한 손으로는
부젓가락 다른 손으로는 망치질을 한다

강철이 처음 대장간에 올 때는 차갑고 뻣뻣했지만
대장간 모루 위에서는 아무리 완강하고 거친 강철이라도
구부러질 수밖에 없다

뜨거운 불속에서 뻘겋게 달궈지고 망치질까지 당하면
강철은 물성이 부드러워진다

한때는 모루와 망치 둘 다 거친 강철이었으나
이제는 그들의 주인과 함께
유용한 물건들을 만들고 있다

Summer High Noon

Abandoned asphalt streets in New York City—nobody walks.
I look out the window where the air shimmers with intense and stifling heat.
The pendulum of the cuckoo clock strikes two.
Everyone in the office slacks off.

A black cat awakens, pulls at his whiskers,
opens its jaws in a teeth-baring yawn, arches its back,
then lies down with outstretched front paws.

The murderous heat comes roll by roll.
Descending like the grasshoppers that invade the streets.
Like a film of gossamer, heat winds around my arm.

Too hot, I don't know whether I breathe or not.
Vigorous heat attacks me thoroughly, through eyes, mouth, armpit and groin.
Uncountable rolls of wrapping heat seal up whole cities.

여름날 정오

아무도 걷지 않는 뉴욕시의 아스팔트 길
나는 창문을 통해 숨 막히게 강한 더위로
펄펄 끓고 있는 반대편 거리를 바라보고 있다
뻐꾸기 시계추가 2시를 알리고 사무실에 있는
모든 사람들은 빈둥대고 있다

검은 고양이가 깨어나 수염을 잡아당기고
턱을 벌려 이빨을 드러내고 하품을 한 다음
등을 구부리고 앞발을 쭉 뻗은 채 드러눕는다

메뚜기 떼가 거리를 습격하듯
살인적 더위가 파도처럼 몰려온다
더위는 가느다란 거미줄 막처럼 내 팔을 감싼다

너무 더워 숨을 쉬고 있는지 모르겠다
폭염이 나의 눈 입 겨드랑이와 사타구니를 덮친다
도시 전체가 무수히 몰려오는 파도 같은
더위에 갇혀버린다

Sign Language

There are few passengers in the afternoon
on the New York City subway.

Save for three young men debating heatedly.
Hands in motion like conductors leading a symphony.

From hands and fingers their words come spewing out rapidly—
soundless into the empty space around them.

Sometimes the men seem to have passionate arguments—
wielding actions that are fast and wide.

They draw circles or straight lines into the empty air.
Clench their fists or open them frequently.

Loosening their hands,
offering encouragement or warning—

I don't know what they are communicating.
But their soundless controversy is continuous.

수화

오후 뉴욕시 지하철에
승객이 거의 없다

교향악 지휘자 같은 손짓을 하면서
열띤 토론을 벌이는 세 명의 젊은이뿐

그들의 말은 그들의 손과 손가락에서 소리 없이
그들 주변의 허공으로 빠르게 분출되고 있다

때로는 한 사람이 빠르고 큰 동작으로
열정적인 주장을 하는 것처럼 보인다

그들은 허공에다 원이나 직선을 그리기도 하고
주먹을 자주 쥐었다 펴기도 한다

손을 늘어뜨려
격려도 하고 경고도 한다

무슨 말을 주고받는지 알 수 없지만
그들의 논쟁은 그칠 줄 모른다

Pedestrian Crosswalk at Times Square

I'm waiting for the traffic light to change to green.
People swarm around me…
clamoring to cross the busy street
within the seven seconds mandated by a machine.

They walk with hurried steps—
students with their smartphones, heads down, watch their screens;
young couples hug, slap and tickle each other;
a whistling young man pulls at his jeans.

A middle-aged woman clutches a purse in one hand
and a fox terrier in another;
an elderly man, wearing large sunglasses hobbles slowly,
while a girl in a wheelchair moves determinedly.

To get to the other side they must move forward quickly—
Going with the flow…moving forward…just forward…
No option for backward motion.
Everyone moving equally.

In this short duration of time, a mass of people,
each with their own style,
moving.

타임스 스퀘어 횡단보도

신호등이 파란불로 바뀌기를 기다린다
사람들이 내 주변에 우르르 몰려 있다
신호등이 길을 건너는 시간을 7초로 제한하고 있어
사람들이 시간 내에 혼잡한 길을 건너려고 북적인다

사람들이 서둘러 걷는다
·학생들은 고개를 숙여 스마트폰 화면을 보면서 걷고
젊은 연인들은 서로 껴안고 때리고 간지럽히며 걷고
휘파람 부는 청년은 자신의 바지를 잡아당기며 걷는다

중년부인은 한손엔 지갑, 다른 손으론 폭스테리어를 안고
건너고
커다란 색안경을 낀 남자노인은 다리를 절며 천천히 걷고
휠체어를 탄 소녀는 결연한 표정으로 휠체어를 움직인다

길 건너편에 도착하려면 그들 모두 신속하게 움직여야 한다
사람의 물결과 함께 앞으로 앞으로만 나아간다
뒤로 움직일 틈이 없다 모두가 같은 방향으로 움직인다

제한된 이 짧은 시간 내에 큰 무리의 사람들이
각자 자신만의 방식으로 움직이고 있다

The Observation Deck of the Empire State Building

The outdoor viewing area is always crowded with visitors.
Tourists gazing through the telescope to the downtown below
or scanning the distant horizon.

Couples in their wedding attire,
pose for their picture,
a bride with a bouquet by the safety fence.

Fathers carry their children on their shoulders
to show them the view
far off into the streets.

One man stands vertically on his friend's shoulder
to see the world from a more high ranking position.

An acrobatic teenager stands upright atop his friend's head.
Stretching his arms he shouts loudly:
"I am the tallest man in the universe!"

Just at that moment a nearby seagull is startled by the sound
and flying away toward the blue sky
evacuates uncontrollably on the deck floor.

엠파이어스테이트 빌딩 전망대

옥외 전망대는 항상 방문객들로 붐빈다
관광객들은 망원경으로 시내를 내려다보거나
저 멀리 수평선을 바라본다

웨딩 복을 입은 신혼부부들이
사진을 찍기 위해 포즈를 취하고 있고
신부 한사람은 부케를 들고 난간에 기대 서있다

아빠들은 아이들이 멀리 시내경치를
볼 수 있도록 목말을 태워준다

한사람은 높은 곳에서 세상을 보려고
친구어깨 위로 수직으로 올라선다

십대 곡예사는 친구 머리 위에 똑바로 서서
팔을 펴고 "내가 우주에서 제일 키 큰 사람이다" 라고
큰 소리로 외친다

그 순간 가까이 있던 갈매기가 외치는 소리에 놀라
전망대 바닥에 똥을 내갈기며
푸른 하늘로 날아오른다

Times Square

A crowded Starbucks has no seats for its customers.
Outside I drink my coffee standing—
a temporary stage in Times Square filled with all kinds of people.

I observe tourists in the busy street: a large crowd jumbled together.
Storytellers, young folks snapping pictures,
an accordion player passing his hat for money,
a bride and bridegroom at their wedding ceremony.

From where I stand it looks like they are all leading incredibly busy lives,
hurrying in step to the building's neon advertisement
that also moves ceaselessly.

Perhaps these people feel as if they are traveling together,
as if they are bewitched
by the flashing pace of billboards.

Among them only the yellow cabs move lazily
through the scurrying crowd of fast walkers.

타임스 스퀘어

붐비는 스타벅스에 자리가 없어 밖으로 나와
혼잡한 거리와 인접한 곳에서 커피를 마신다

타임스 스퀘어의 가설무대는 모든 종류의 사람들로 붐빈다
관광객들 요란한 문신을 한 사람들 사진을 찍어 대는
젊은이들
모금용 모자를 돌리는 아코디언 연주자
결혼식을 올리는 신랑신부도 보인다

거리의 인파는 차량과 행인들과 뒤섞인다
사람들은 매우 서두르며 믿을 수 없을 만큼
바쁘게 살고 있는 것 같다

사람들은 그들만큼이나 끊임없이 움직이는
건물의 네온사인 광고를 향해 종종걸음을 한다
아마도 광고판에 넋이 나가 광고판과 함께
여행을 떠나는 착각에 빠진 것 같다

오직 노란색 영업용 택시만이 종종걸음 걷는
사람들 사이를 느리게 움직이고 있다

Cigarette Butts

Scattered at random on the ground.
Each body crumpled with different forms.

Broken and cracked.
The numerous teeth marks
and lipstick stains remain

ugly on the bodies.
Marks on marks,
scars on scars.

Enduring the pain of constant biting.
Keeping all of the stories of hardship within,
their small bodies never forgetting.

Once the smokers' best friends,
They are now weltered and trampled
by pedestrians.

Cigarettes made dizzy by smoke from cherry lips,
fascinated with fragrances.
They gave fealty to their master.

Gone now.
Cast off!

They are quietly waiting
to decompose.
Perhaps strike up again.

꽁초

여러 가지 모양으로 구겨진 꽁초들이
땅바닥에 아무렇게나 흩어져 있다

부러지고 갈라진 꽁초들에는
수많은 이빨자국이 나 있고 입술연지도 묻어 있다

추한 모습인데다 흔적 위에 흔적이 있고
자국 위에 자국이 있다

계속 씹히는 고통을 견뎌내야 했고
속으로 겪었던 힘든 사연을 모두 간직하고 있기에
꽁초는 결코 잊을 수가 없다

한때는 흡연자들의 가장 친한 친구였으나
이제는 행인들에 의해 짓밟혀 굴러다닌다

담배들은 체리 입술에서
나오는 연기에 현기증을 느꼈고
향기에 매료되었다
그들은 주인에게 충성을 다 바쳤다

이제 끝났어
던져버려!

꽁초들은 조용히 썩을 때를 기다린다
아마도 새 담배에 불을 붙이겠지

Diving

Because it is too hot, I eat a lot of cold watermelon
adjust my easy chair all the way back
take a rest while listening to classical music.

We fling off our clothes—even our underpants—and dive into the river.
The water so soothing cool and crystal clear
we can see the bottom.

I am swimming with dear old friends
who live in the rural village
of my homeland in Korea.

We have a contest to see who will be the first to cross the river,
who can stay longest underwater without breathing,
who is the fastest, strongest, the one with most endurance.

I climb a rock near the river
spread out my arms like an angel
and leap off.

I fall down
bumping my head
on the carpeted floor
of my living room.

다이빙

너무나 더워 차가운 수박을 많이 먹고
안락의자를 끝까지 뒤로 넘겨
휴식을 취하며 클래식음악을 듣는다

옷과 내의까지 벗어 던지고 물속으로 뛰어든다
수정같이 맑은 물이 내 몸을 포근히 감싸준다

나는 내 조국 코리아의 시골마을에서
정든 옛 친구들과 수영을 하고 있다

우리는 누가 먼저 강을 헤엄쳐 건너는지
누가 물속에서 숨을 오래 참고 견디는지
누가 가장 빠르고 강하고 인내력 있는지 경쟁을 한다

나는 강 근처에 있는 바위로 올라가
팔을 천사의 날개처럼 벌리고 뛰어내린다

나는 양탄자 깔린 내 거실 바닥에
머리를 부딪치고 쓰러진다

The Rosary

In the relics' exhibition of the antiquated abbey, a rosary is displayed.
All beads threaded onto a string at regular distances;
tight knots of the cord decoupled so there is an intimacy
among the bodies of the beads.

Faded beads show traces of the time and tide.
Well-thumbed wooden beads shine in dim light.
Gold beads seem to murmur something I cannot comprehend.

Alongside these compelling strands my eyes
alight upon a woman's portrait.
Though she is gone,
her boundless prayers seem to continue through the ages.

These beads—like a life partner—cherish many of her wishes,
remember the fervent prayers spoken during worship to her God.
Perhaps her earnest desires not only came to nothing,
but were returned with despair.

If the beads spoke to me they would tell of the many tears
that appeared in her eyes.
How a new crucifix attached to the rosary
was bright when she first used it—
Then suddenly, beads are left alone, abandoned.

묵주

고대 수도원 유물전시관에는 묵주들이 줄줄이 전시돼 있다
묵주 알들이 일정한 간격으로 줄에 꿰어져 있고
묵주 알들 사이에 일정한 간격을 유지하기 위해
다른 한 쪽 끈에는 단단한 매듭들을 만들어 놓았다

변색된 묵주 알들은 세월의 흔적을 말해준다
손때가 묻은 묵주 알들이 희미한 빛을 받아 반짝인다
진열장 안에 있는 묵주 알들은 내가 알아듣지 못하는
무언가를 속삭이는 듯하다

한 여인의 초상화가 눈에 번쩍 띄었다
묵주 한 개가 그녀의 초상화 옆에 놓여있다
그녀는 떠나갔지만 그녀의 기도는 세월이 가도
변함없이 계속되고 있는 것 같다

이 묵주 알들은 그녀와 평생을 함께했기에 그녀가 빌었던
여러 소원들을 고이 간직하고 있을 것이다
그녀가 하나님께 기도드릴 때 그녀가 했던 기도
그리고 그녀가 뜨겁게 염원했던 욕망들이 물거품이 되고
그 욕망들로 인해 그녀가 오히려 절망에 빠진 것을
기억하고 있을 것이다

만일 이 묵주들이 말을 할 수 있다면
살아생전 그녀의 눈에 맺혔던 수많은
눈물방울들에 관한 이야기도 해 줄 것이다
묵주에 달린 새 십자가가 처음에는 얼마나 반짝거렸는지
그리고 어느 날 갑자기 그녀가 떠나고 묵주만
홀로 남아 버려지게 되었는지를

At the Margaret Mitchell House in Atlanta

Under the calm light her framed picture kindly welcomes visitors.
A typewriter holds a paper with words captured on half a page.

Cannons from the Civil War faintly thunder from the old machine.
But those sounds are drowned out for a time by a guide who recounts her life.

I meet Scarlet O'Hara in another hanging picture frame.
She welcomes me with a smile; seems to say that tomorrow is another day.

I nod gently to the portrait,
fighting the impulse to wind the spring that would awaken
the old phonograph player.

The bed and sofa in the room hint of the leisure in her life.
The cooking pots, spoons, forks and knives reveal
the kitchen customs of those days.

In the course of looking around at the past, I wander to the exit door,
and my mind abruptly returns to the present.

애틀랜타 마가렛 미첼 생가에서

차분한 조명아래 액자 속 작가의 사진이 방문객을 반긴다
반 페이지쯤 타이핑된 원고가 물려 있는 타자기

오래된 타자기에서 남북전쟁의 포성이 울려오다가
작가의 생애를 설명하는 가이드의 해설소리에 잠시
중단된다

나는 다른 액자에 담긴 스칼렛 오하라를 만난다
그녀는 나를 반기며 내일에는 새로운 날이 온다고 말한다

나는 구식 축음기 소리를 듣기위해 태엽을 감고 싶은
충동을 억제하며 그녀의 초상에 정중히 목례를 한다

방안에 있는 침대와 소파는 안락했던 그녀의 삶을 보여주고
냄비 스푼 포크 나이프 등은 당시의 요리 관습을 보여준다

과거를 둘러보면서 이리저리 걷다가 출구로 나오니
내 마음은 획하고 현재로 돌아온다

At a Shopping Mall

In New York City my wife and I go together to the shopping mall.
With all its enticements
it seems to be waiting for customers.

We are poor country people though.
Not familiar with malls.
So we step slowly through the stores.

We push our large cart and look
with our eyes opened wide...
hunting for a discount corner
to purchase goods with a big sale price.

My wife shows an interest in buying kitchen appliances—
white porcelain tea pots, pottery jars and stainless steel pans.
Items she always longed to have
in our kitchen at home in Korea.

But on this occasion I try to calm her earnest desires.
Telling her that we could buy
the more expensive items
next time.

Then my wife scolds me vehemently
about a next time that is coming continually
again and again
and never arrives.

쇼핑몰에서

아내와 함께 뉴욕시에 있는 쇼핑몰에 간다
쇼핑몰은 온갖 것들로 유혹을 하며
고객을 기다린다

우리는 가난한 나라 사람들이라
쇼핑몰에 익숙하지 않아
상점들을 천천히 걸어서 지나간다

큰 카트를 밀고 할인 폭이 큰 물건을
살 수 있는 할인코너를 눈을 크게 뜨고 찾는다

아내는 고국의 고향집에서 항상 갖고 싶어 했던
백자 찻잔 도자기병 스테인리스 냄비 같은
주방용품을 사는데 관심을 보인다

그러나 나는 다음번에 더 비싼 걸 사자고
그녀를 설득해 그녀의 간절한 욕구를
이번에는 가라앉힌다

그러자 아내는 다음번은 오고 또 오고
계속된다고 나를 심히 나무랐다

Aged Dartboard at the Flea Market

Every Saturday I visit the flea market.
Even when snow flurries slide in through the open showcase.
Every gust of wind shaking the portable tent, the old Lespedeza door.

Today I find an aged dartboard hung on a makeshift wall.
Its surface color faded and partially flaked off.
Most of the numbers only dimly visible.

There are places that illustrate the history
where passionate players once competed.
Aiming the dart at the marked lucky numbers to win the game.

But the board holds both lucky and unlucky numbers
and though everyone sets sights on the inner bull's-eye
it is difficult to hit the mark.

Now remember the players of long ago,
their jubilant and wistful smiles, win or lose.

Now the old salesman's wrinkled face
feels the cold winds passing through
the lonely ether.

벼룩시장에서 발견한 낡은 다트 게임 판

나는 매주 토요일 벼룩시장을 찾는다
행사장에 눈이 흩날려 내릴 때도 마찬가지다
한바탕 바람이 불면 휴대용 텐트가 펄럭이고 싸리문이
흔들린다

오늘은 임시로 만든 벽에 걸린 낡은 다트 게임 판을
발견한다
판은 퇴색됐고 부분적으로 벗겨져 있다
대부분의 숫자들은 희미하게만 보일 뿐이다

한 때 사람들이 게임에 이기기 위해
이 판에 표시된 행운의 숫자에
화살을 조준하며 열정적으로 게임을 했을 것이다

그러나 다트 게임 판에는 행운의 숫자와 불운의 숫자가
함께 표시되어 있어 모두가 정통으로 맞추려 조준을 해도
과녁을 맞히기가 쉽지 않았을 것이다

오래 전 다트게임을 했던 사람들을 기억하라
그들이 이겼을 때 지었던 기쁨 가득한 웃음과
졌을 때 지었던 아쉬움 가득한 웃음을 기억하라

이제는 늙어 주름진 세일즈맨의 얼굴에
하늘에서 바람이 불어오고 있다

Journey With No Definite Objective

In a rural park I sit on a sloped wooden bench,
make a pillow of my arm for my head,
gaze up at the distant sky, lost in thought.

There are nine hundred lambs and one thousand swans
walking at a leisurely pace in line across the sky.
A faint crescent moon hangs between them.

A shepherd in white clothes with a staff in his hand follows slowly.
Sometimes the staff pokes its head into the crescent pulling it up
toward the herd of lambs.

There is no traffic cop or expert to expedite these movements, to
make sure that everything flows harmoniously.

Two groups of white birds high in the sky turn round and round,
their feathers floating on wind that seems lighter than air.

All of them drift toward me—lambs, swans and birds.
Balanced buoyantly on a journey
with no definite objective.

정처 없는 여행

시골공원 경사진 목재 벤치에 앉아
팔베개를 하고 먼 하늘을 바라보며
생각에 잠긴다

하늘에는 구백 마리의 양과 천 마리의 백조가
일렬로 느릿느릿 걷고 있고
그들 사이에는 희미한 초승달이 걸려있다

손에 지팡이를 든 흰 옷 입은 목동이
천천히 뒤따르는데 지팡이 머리 부분이
간간히 초승달을 찌르며
달을 양떼 쪽으로 끌어당긴다

교통순경도 없고 모두가 조화를 이뤄
원활하게 흘러가게 해줄 전문가도 없다

바람을 타고 공기보다 더 가벼워 보이는
날개를 가진 두 떼의 새들이
하늘 높은 곳에서 빙빙 돌고 있다

두둥실 떠도는 정처 없는 여행길에서
제대로 모양을 갖춘 양과 백조와 새들이
모두 내게로 흘러온다

Panorama of the Streets

Autumn breezes
blow the yellow leaves
off the roadside trees.
They scatter on the asphalt pavement.

A surging crowd of leaves are rambling through the streets
according to the winds.
They all fade to a similar color,
trampled down by shoes and tires recklessly.
My trousers brush past some of these lean leaves.

No one shows an interest in them.
Except an old woman at the bus stop
examining them carefully.
She seems to long for the vibrant colors and glorious times
of the past.

In the street so many people gather.
The surging crowds are moved around
here and there, according to the traffic lights.

Where do they come from? When?
How long will they be wandering from place to place?
Did the leaves, like them, have days of youth?

The buses come and go.
The old woman departs and others appear.
Afterward autumn leaves disappear from here.
The roadside trees will come into bud next spring.

In the night the crowds will be buried in darkness.
What is seen today is gone with the night.
Yet the panorama of the streets of New York
will remain with me for a long time to come.

거리 풍경

가을 산들바람이 가로수 잎을 날려
아스팔트위로 흩어지게 한다

낙엽더미들이 바람 따라 거리에 몰려다니고 있다
낙엽들은 비슷비슷한 색깔로 변해 사람들의 발과
자동차 바퀴에 아무렇게나 짓밟히고 있다
얇은 낙엽들이 나의 바지에도 스친다

버스정거장에서 할머니 한 분이 낙엽을 유심히
바라볼 뿐 낙엽에 관심을 갖는 사람이 없다
할머니는 지난날 생기발랄하고 눈부시게 아름답던 때를
그리워하는 것 같다

거리에는 많은 사람들이 교통신호에 따라
이리저리 움직인다

이 사람들은 어디에서 온 것일까 그리고 언제 온 것일까
그리고 사람들은 얼마동안 이리저리 돌아다닐까
이 사람들에게도 낙엽처럼 젊은 날이 있었을까

버스가 오가고 있다
할머니가 떠나고 다른 사람들이 나타난다
가을 낙엽은 얼마 후 이곳에서 사라질 것이다
내년 봄이 오면 가로수에는 새싹이 돋아날 것이다

밤에는 낙엽의 무리들이 어둠에 묻힐 것이다
내가 오늘 보고 있는 것들은 밤과 함께 사라질 것이다
그러나 뉴욕 전경은 오랫동안 내 가슴에
남아 있을 것 같다

On Breezy Waikiki Beach

The rainbows sing.
Sky is high through a rift in the clouds.
Too many waves to count.
Too much sand to count.
Too many days to count.

White birds skim over the sea.
Sailboards skim the calm sea.
So many colorful parasols!
Young people surfing.
Bikini-clad sunbathers.

While waves talk with sand,
rainbows, clouds, and wind,
Hawaiians drum and dance.
Like sighing for the good old days
the stories are continued with murmuring waves.

If I were wind I could hear you.

If I should meet you again after a long time, Waikiki,
how should I greet you?

미풍이 부는 와이키키 해변에서

무지개가 노래한다
구름 사이로 하늘이 높다
헤아릴 수 없이 많은 파도
헤아릴 수 없이 많은 모래
헤아릴 수 없이 많은 날들

하얀 새들이 바다 위를 스치며 난다
돛단배들은 고요한 바다를 미끄러지듯 항해한다
무수히 많은 여러 색깔의 파라솔들
젊은이들은 서핑을 하고 비키니 입은 사람들은 일광욕을 한다

하얀 파도가 모래, 무지개, 구름 바람과 대화를 하는 동안
하와이사람들은 북을 치고 춤을 춘다
옛날이 그리워 한숨을 쉬듯
소곤대는 파도 소리 속에 이야기는 계속된다

내가 바람이라면
네 말을 들을 수 있을 텐데

와이키키여
오랜 세월 지나 널 다시 만난다면
어떤 식으로 인사를 하게 될까

Dream of a Marathon Runner

Marathon athletes at the starting line in the bright sunshine
of the London 2012 Olympics. Ready to run the course:
past Buckingham Palace, St. Paul's Cathedral, the Tower of London.

Tagged on their front and rear with a name and an ID number.
After long hard years of training they stand
as representatives of their country.

As soon as the signal is sounded their journey begins.
Sturdy legs propel them toward the finish line. They compete.
Hoping to accomplish a dream.

At the signal
some runners rush forward to the head of the pack.
But their lead begins to shrink after half the course is run.

The day grows hotter.

Some runners drink too much water
from the bottles offered along the way.

Some runners look often at their watches.
Only at last to give up on their journey.

Although racing brings their bodies together,
the struggle for survival is a solitary pursuit.

One runner controls his pace with precision—
suddenly surges ahead in the final stages of the race.
Leaping like a stag from inside the pack to the front position.

Winning the race.
He becomes the gold medalist.
Draped in his country's flag.

At the finish line
the last runner to cross tells the press,
"The journey is more important than the medals.
Never giving up along the way, is the final achievement."

어떤 마라톤 선수의 꿈

화창한 날씨 속에 2012년 런던 올림픽 출발선에 선
마라톤 선수들 앞과 뒤에 이름과 번호를 달고
버킹엄궁전 성 바오로 성당과 런던탑을
지나가는 코스를 달릴 준비를 마쳤다

힘들고 오랜 훈련을 마치고 선수들은
그들의 조국을 대표해 출발선에 서 있다

출발신호가 울리자 그들의 여정은 시작된다
건각의 선수들이 결승선을 향해 달려간다
선수들은 그들의 꿈을 이루기 위해 경쟁한다

출발신호가 울리자 일부 선수들은 선두그룹으로 나선다
그러나 코스의 절반이 지났을 때는
선두그룹과 다음그룹의 간격이 줄어든다.

날씨는 점점 더워지고
일부 선수들은 길가에서 제공되는
물을 너무 많이 마신다

일부 선수들은 시계를 자주 보다가
결국에 가서는 경기를 포기한다

마라톤 경기에서 선수들은 함께 뛰지만
살기 위해서는 혼자 투쟁해야 한다

무리 속에 함께 있다 선두로 나서는 수사슴처럼
한 선수가 경기 막판에 페이스를 정확하게 조절한
후 갑자기 앞으로 튀어나온다

우승을 한 그 선수는 금메달을 따고
자기나라 국기를 몸에 두른다

마지막 선수가 결승선을 통과하고 나서
취재진에게 말한다
 "메달보다 여정이 더 중요하다
중도에 포기하지 않는 자가 최종 승리자다."

Dreaming Each Day

What did you do today? If you ask me this, I did nothing.
What did you do today? If you ask again, I did too much.
I do something every day, but don't know exactly what it is.
I do nothing every day, but too busy always.

What do I gain day-to-day? I don't know.
The sun rises and the sun sets, but I don't perceive it.
There are so many stars in the sky, but I cannot count them,
unless I let myself fall into evening.

Waves in the ocean, sands on the beach, leaves in the forest,
days of our life,
How many numbers are they?
Is it utterly meaningless to talk about?

In order to know them, I'm living.

I get up every morning,
work for my livelihood,
and I cultivate myself each day.

Descartes said, *I think, therefore I am*, and they are.
From nine to five, morning to evening,
I am wasting away outwardly, but
I am renewed inwardly day by day.

Even though I am a mist that appears
for a little while and vanishes,
I don't lose heart.

For my light and momentary troubles
are ripening
a beautiful dream.

I cultivate myself each day.
I dream the dream each day.

매일 꿈을 꾸며

오늘은 무얼 했습니까? 라고 묻는다면
나는 아무것도 한 게 없습니다
오늘은 무얼 했습니까? 라고 다시 묻는다면
나는 너무나 많은 일을 했습니다
나는 매일 무언가를 하지만 그게 정확히 무엇인지 모릅니다
나는 매일 아무것도 안 하지만 항상 너무 바쁩니다

날이면 날마다 얻는 게 뭐냐구요? 모르겠습니다
해가 뜨고 지지만 나는 그걸 감지하지 못합니다
하늘에는 별들이 많지만 나는 저녁 속에 빠져들지 않으면
그것들을 셀 수 없습니다

바다의 파도, 해변의 모래, 숲 속의 나뭇잎, 우리 인생의
날들
헤아려 보면 그 숫자가 얼마나 될까요?
숫자를 논하는 것은 무의미한 일일까요?

그 것들을 알아보기 위해
나는 지금 살고 있습니다

나는 매일 아침에 일어나
생계를 위해 일하고 나 자신을 가꿉니다

데카르트는 "나는 *생각한다. 고로 나는 존재한다.*"
라고 말했습니다
나는 겉으로는 낡아지고 있지만
안으로는 매일 새로워지고 있습니다

내가 비록 잠깐 나타났다 사라지는
안개라 해도 낙심하지 않습니다

나의 소소하고 일시적인 고난들이
나의 아름다운 꿈을 키워주기에

나는 매일 꿈을 꾸며
나 자신을 가꿉니다

Refugees

Like fallen leaves that sway in the wind
shadowed by scattered clouds
we wander from place to place
taking steps wherever our legs might carry us.

Not staying regularly in any one place
we never know where we should stop for sleep.
We are afraid of darkness.

We never knew that people could be so callous
the morning dew so cold
and early frost is hard as stone.

In the old days we didn't recognize
that worthless fog was important—
wrapping us out of sight
creating a kindly feeling
even though we shivered with cold.

We are fallen leaves
discarded by trees
in front of our own houses—

Houses that are run down and abandoned.
Leaves that are strewn about by the winds.

난민

바람에 나부끼는 낙엽처럼
조각구름 그림자에 가린 것처럼
발길 닿는 대로 이곳저곳을 떠돈다

어느 한 곳에 정기적으로 머물 수 없고
어디서 잠을 잘지 알 수도 없으니
밤이 오는 게 두렵구나

세상이 그토록 냉혹하고
아침이슬이 그렇게 차갑고
이른 서리가 그렇게
돌처럼 단단한 줄 몰랐다

쓸모 없다고 생각했던 안개가
우리를 추위에 떨게 해도
우리 모습을 감춰주고
포근하게 대해주는
중요한 존재라는 것을 미처 몰랐다

우리는 쓰러지고 방치된
우리의 집들 앞 나무에서 떨어져
황폐해 버려진 후 바람에 이리저리
흩어지는 낙엽이다

Last Hope for Dreams

What force causes a young boy to be drowned at sea?
The image on my T.V. captures him face down in the sand,
broken waves sweeping over him continuously.

Refugees in mass migrations—
like butterflies or birds, tenuous, fragile,
resting in the streets, frantic facing starvation
or arrest by militia.

A young child walks barefoot over cold stone slabs.
A mother with belongings bundled on her head
holds a child in each hand.
These Internet images I see…

Desperate to cross a border of mesh wire fence
into neighboring country or further
guarded by frontier garrison
pushed back, brutally beaten.

Even though they are hard-pressed on every side
they fix their dream not on what is seen
but on what is unseen.

꿈을 향한 마지막 희망

어떤 폭력이 어린 소년을 바다에 익사시켰는가
TV 영상을 보니 모래밭에 엎드린 소년의 시신 위로
파도가 부서지며 쉴 새 없이 덮치고 있다

보잘것없고 나약한 나비들이나 새들처럼
길에서 쉬고 굶주림에 허덕이다
민병대에 체포되는 집단이주 난민들

맨발의 어린애가 차가운 석판 위를 걷고
엄마는 소지품을 한데 묶어 머리에 이고
양손에는 두 아이의 손을 잡고 있는 것을
인터넷에서 본다

그물철망 국경을 필사적으로 넘어
이웃나라나 그 다음나라로 가려다
수비대의 감시를 받고 추방되거나
가혹하게 구타당하는 난민들

모든 면에서 심한 압박을 받아도
그들은 보이는 것이 아니라
보이지 않는 것에 희망을 걸고 있다

An Empty Space

When a woman volunteer approaches an orphan at the refugee village
a boy opens his arms and tightly hugs her.

Like a magnet the boy clings to her and won't let go.
Other orphans clamber to her, but there is no room for them.

Watching this on my television screen
I see a huge unfilled place between them.

And the empty spaces in the eyes of each orphan
like an abyss of sorrow and despair.

Who can make smaller
these barren spaces between them?

빈 공간

한 여성 자원봉사자가 난민촌에서
어떤 고아에게 다가가니
한 소년이 팔을 벌리고
그녀를 꼭 껴안는다

그 소년은 자석처럼 그녀에게 달라붙어
그녀를 놔주지 않고 다른 고아들도 그녀에게
기어올라보지만 더 안아줄 여유가 없다

TV 화면에 비친 아이들 간에는 채워지지 않는
커다란 빈자리가 있고

그들의 눈에는 슬픔과 절망의 심연 같은
빈 공간이 있음을 본다

그들 사이에 존재하는 이 척박한 공간을
누가 좁혀줄 것인가?

III.

The Seasons Have Gone But....

The seasons revolve,
and the years change unconsciously
without asking or notice.

The light green grass in the fields that comes up through the ground decorates
the wildflowers. The shimmering spring heat waving in the air
helps bloom the flowers of the peach and azalea.
Will my hometown also bloom by now?

The town I lived in was the flowering mountain in the spring.
Even though I now live in distant lands far away,
the flowers that bloom in my heart are aflutter
with the idea of returning there.

You were only laughing silently about that time;
the petals of those days were tinted with shyness.
Though far away, it continues to haunt me.

The seasons, without taking thought,
revolve in cycles—spring, summer, autumn, and winter.
The seasons that have been forgotten
have come back with nostalgia,
and you are full in my heart of vast vacancy.

The turning seasons each time put fire on the wick of a forgotten longing.
Past seasons have gone,
but those days remain in my heart.

My heart set on what I have been longing for,
while the moon moves in its cycle—crescent, half moon, full.
The flower petals too have bloomed and fallen
but your shy smile is unchanged.

계절은 지나가지만

계절은 순환하고
해는 묻지도 않고 예고도 없이
무심결에 바뀐다

땅에 돋아난 연초록 풀들이
야생화를 돋보이게 해준다
아롱대는 봄의 열기가
배꽃과 진달래꽃을 피게 한다
내 고향에도 꽃이 피고있을까

내 고향은 봄이면 꽃이 피는 산골이었다
지금은 먼 나라에 와 살고 있지만
내 가슴에 핀 꽃은
고향에 돌아갈 생각에 들떠 있다

그때 그대는 조용히 웃고만 있었지만
그때 꽃잎들은 수줍은 빛을 띠고 있었다
멀리 떨어져 사는 지금도 자주 회상한다

무심한 계절은 봄여름 가을 겨울 순으로 바뀐다
잊었던 계절이 찾아와 향수를 불러일으키면
텅 빈 내 가슴은 당신으로 가득 찬다

계절은 바뀔 때마다 잊었던 그리움의 심지에
매번 불을 붙이고 계절은 가도
그리운 날들은 가슴에 남는다

달은 초승달 반달 보름달로 주기적으로 변해도
그리움은 내 가슴에 변함없이 남아있고
꽃잎은 피었다 졌어도
그대의 수줍은 미소는 변함없이 남아있다

Opening Night, Predawn Morning

In the new opera house, so elegant and clean,
my wife and I sit together.
My heart flutters in anticipation.

We are so poor we can only afford seats under the balcony.
Our view is obscured, but it is enough that we can still fly away to
curious countries through the stories conjured during the performance.

The orchestra's overture blares out
toward both sides of the curtain moving slowly.
And the brilliant stars on stage lead us to a new world.

Before daylight on the mountain in the foreground of my village
the merry chatter of the sparrows
wake the livestock and the reed forest from a sound sleep.

With each new day I always expect a new possibility.
The curtain of night pulling back,
a radiant sun dawning over the mountain ridge inch by inch,
opening up a new world brightly.

A world that I sincerely welcome
each new day
with my arms open wide
taking a bow, receiving applause.

개막일 밤과 동트는 아침

품격 있고 깨끗한 오페라극장에
아내와 함께 앉아있으니
기대감으로 가슴이 설렌다

형편이 넉넉하지 못한 우리는
발코니 아래 좌석의 표를 샀다
어렴풋이 보여도 공연 중 드러나는 이야기를 통해
궁금한 나라들에 가볼 수 있으니 상관이 없다

오페라 서곡이 서서히 움직이는 커튼의 양쪽으로
우렁차게 울려 나오고 빛나는 스타들이 무대에서
우리를 신세계로 안내한다

해뜨기 전 고향마을 앞산의 참새들이
즐겁게 지저귀는 소리가
가축들과 갈대숲을 깊은 잠에서 깨운다

하루가 새로 시작될 때마다
나는 새로운 가능성을 기대한다
밤의 커튼이 거두어 지면 빛나는 태양이 산 너머에서
서서히 새로운 세상을 밝게 열어준다

나는 두 팔을 활짝 펴고 갈채와 박수를 받으며
매일 새로운 세상을 기쁜 마음으로 영접한다

Arirang

With much mirth at the party we are singing Arirang.
"Why are you always singing Arirang?" our children ask."
Because it heals our nostalgia for our homeland."

Arirang, Arirang, Arariyo...
(Arirang, Arirang, Arariyo...)
You are going over Arirang hill.
(Arirang gogaero neomeoganda.)

My love, you are leaving me
(Nareul beorigo gasineun nimeun)
Your feet will be sore before you go ten ri.
(Sibrido mosgaseo balbyeongnanda.)

The Arirang song; our unofficial national anthem,
our favorite chorus, our best friend and coordinator
in the people's party of the homeland.

Just as there are many stars in the clear sky,
(Cheongcheonhaneuren janbyeoldo manko,)
There are also many dreams in our heart.
(Urine gaseumen huimangdo manda.)

There, over there, that mountain is Baekdu Mountain,
(Jeogi jeo sani Baekdusaniraji,)
Where, even in the middle of winter days, flowers bloom.
(Dongji seotdaredo kkotman pinda.)

We begin to dance a Korean folk dance
to the melody of the Arirang...
We dance with both hands,

sometimes holding a handkerchief in one hand,
the other hand resting on the waist,
dancing forward and backward repeatedly.

아리랑

우리는 파티에서 즐겁게 아리랑을 부른다
아이들이 "왜 항상 아리랑을 불러요?" 하고 묻는다
"아리랑이 고국에 대한 향수를 달래주기 때문이야"

아리랑, 아리랑, 아라리요...
아리랑 고개로 넘어간다.

나를 버리고 가시는 님은
십리도 못 가서 발병난다.

아리랑은 우리나라의 비공식 국가
가장 사랑하는 합창곡
우리의 절친 고국 민중의 중재자

청천하늘엔 잔별도 많고,
우리네 가슴엔 희망도 많다.

저기 저 산이 백두산이라지,
동지 섣달에도 꽃만 핀다.

우리는 두 손으로 아리랑 곡조에 맞춰
때로는 한손으로 손수건을 흔들고

다른 한 손은 허리에 갖다 대고
앞으로 뒤로 왔다 갔다를 반복하는
우리의 전통 춤을 추기 시작한다

We toast to our success and health.
We form a ring and dance, again and again and again…
we spin right to left, then the opposite way, singing the chorus merrily.

Arirang, Arirang, Arariyo…
(Arirang, Arirang, Arariyo…)
You are going over Arirang hill.
(Arirang gogaero neomeoganda.)

* "**Arirang**" is a Korean folk song, often considered the unofficial national
anthem of Korea. There are about 3,600 variations of 60 different versions
of the song, all of which include a refrain similar to, *Arirang, arirang, arariyo.*
It is estimated the song is more than 600 years old.

우리는 우리의 성공과 건강에 건배를 하고
동그란 원을 만들어 왼쪽으로 돌다가
다시 반대로 돌기도 하면서
즐거운 합창과 함께 춤을 추고 또 춘다

아리랑, 아리랑, 아라리요...
아리랑 고개로 넘어간다.

*** 아리랑은 코리아의 민요이며 비공식 국가로 간주된다.
60가지 버전과 약 3,000가지 종류가 있다. 노래가 모두
"아리랑, 아리랑, 아라리요" 와 같이 유사한 후렴을
포함한다.
노래가 600년 넘는 동안 전해진 것으로 추정된다.

Flower Watch

I return to my home country of Korea—
Walk along the riverside where clovers grow
where Seunee and I played together as children.
We were poor, but happy.

Sometimes we squatted in the clover fields
searching for four-leaf clovers all day long
—believing it might bring us luck.
But it was not easy to find this treasure.

Sometimes we bet on who would discover a four-leaf clover first;
but Seunee always won.
Sometimes she asked me to sing to her or kiss her cheek.
Or make a watch from the clover flowers to adorn her wrist.

At first I didn't know how to create this thing.
But I soon realized that to make one watch
two flowers must be equally joined together.

Now I stand alone in the vast clover plains
in the dusk where flowers are in full bloom.
I call for Seunee loudly, but there is no answer.
Only a lonely echo.

꽃 손목시계

나는 내 조국 코리아로 돌아간다
순이와 내가 가난해도 행복했던 어린 시절
함께 놀던 클로버 무성했던 강변을 걷는다

종종 우리는 온종일 클로버 밭에 쭈그리고 앉아
네 잎 클로버가 행운을 가져다 줄 것이라 믿으며
네 잎 클로버를 찾았지만 쉽지 않았다

때로는 누가 먼저 네 잎 클로버를 찾는지
내기를 했고 그때마다 순이가 나를 이겼다
때로는 순이가 나에게 노래를 불러 달라 했고
그녀의 뺨에 키스를 해달라고도 했고
클로버로 꽃시계를 만들어 손목에 채워달라고도 했다

처음에 나는 꽃시계를 어떻게 만들 줄 몰랐으나
두개의 꽃을 똑같이 연결하면 된다는 걸 알게 됐다

이제 어둠 속 꽃이 만발한 클로버 밭에 홀로 서서
순이의 이름을 소리 내어 불러봐도 대답은 없고
외로운 메아리만 울려 퍼진다

At the Gate

I stop by chance at the gate of my childhood home.
It is dusk. More than fifty years have passed away.

I can only see the roof of the house that is surrounded by a high wall,
and I don't know who is living there.

Now I imagine that someone is about to come running to me.
Shouting my name for joy.

The thatched roof has been tiled
and the wooden fence—overgrown with clover—
has become a blunt concrete wall.

Inside the courtyard, the Evergreens have disappeared
and the cold wind sweeps through its empty space.

I hesitate a moment, deliberate, whether to push the gate's bell.
Then I give up and close my eyes. Sit with my back against the wall.

Now childhood friends are singing the folk ballads of long ago.
The songs echo through the icicles hanging
from the eaves of the straw roof.

One by one the faces of loved ones flash through my mind.
Those good old days have ascended high up into the sky
and dispersed like meteors.

옛집 앞에서

저녁 무렵 우연히 어린 시절 살던 집 대문에 멈춰 선다
50년이 넘는 세월이 흘러갔다

높은 벽으로 둘러싸여 지붕만 보이는 집에
지금은 누가 살고 있는지 알 수 없지만
누군가가 금방 내 이름을 부르며 달려 나올 것 같다

초가지붕은 타일로 바뀌었고
클로버가 무성하던 목재 담장은 뭉툭한 시멘트벽으로
바뀌었다
마당에 있던 사철 푸르던 소나무는 사라졌고 그 텅 빈
공간을
찬바람이 휩쓸고 지나간다

나는 잠시 머뭇거리다 대문의 초인종을 누를지 말지
생각한다
그러나 포기하고서는 눈을 감고 등을 벽에 기대어 앉는다

지금 나의 어릴 적 친구들이 옛 노래를 부르고 있다
노래 소리는 초가지붕 처마에 매달린 고드름을 지나 메아리
친다
사랑했던 사람들의 얼굴이 하나 둘씩 떠오른다
정답던 그 시절은 하늘로 올라가 유성처럼 흩어지고 말았다

Come Back Soon

Wed during the Korean War,
a marriage night of ecstasy, the nuptial bed, a bliss…
and at that very moment an explosion.

Startled, the bridegroom cries out!
Sweeps aside his bride, leaving her behind in the room.
Saying, *"I'll come back soon."*

She firmly believes that he will be back at once.
Remains awake all night waiting.
Although no information ever comes,
the bride waits for him, faithfully.

She remains in their old house,
not moving to another place, or city.
Not wanting to repair anything broken,
even to exchange the gate for a new one.

She fears that her husband might not recognize the house
with its thatched straw roof
that they had entered
the first night of matrimony.

Almost sixty years later,
the old bridegroom visits his hometown on business
after getting government approval.

By now he has forgotten his first wife
but still curious about the old house
he stops there spontaneously.

When she opens the door, the old bride recognizes her husband.
Her heart flutters greatly.
She becomes a white balloon.

And when the old bridegroom touches her
her heart fills with so much compassion
she floats up into the sky.

곧 돌아와요

한반도 전쟁 나던 해 결혼, 황홀한 첫날밤, 신혼침대,
더 없는 행복... 바로 그 순간 터지는 폭발음

신랑은 놀라 외치며 신부를 옆으로 밀쳐내고
"곧 돌아올 게요" 한 마디하고 신부를 떠나간다

그녀는 그가 곧 돌아올 거라 굳게 믿으며
밤새도록 자지 않고 기다린다
아무 소식이 없어도 그녀는 충직하게 기다린다

그녀는 결혼 첫날밤 그들이 함께 머물던
초가집을 그녀의 남편이 찾지 못할까 봐

그 집에 홀로 남아 다른 주소나
다른 도시로 이사도 하지 않고
부서진 곳이 생겨도 고치지도 않고
대문도 새것으로 바꾸지 않는다

거의 60년이 지난 후 나이가 든 신랑이
정부승인을 받아 자신의 고향집을 방문한다

이때 신랑은 그의 첫째 부인의 존재를 잊은 채
옛집이 궁금한 나머지 방문을 한다

그때 그녀가 문을 열고 신랑을 알아본다
그녀는 가슴이 크게 설레는 하얀 풍선

나이든 신랑이 그녀를 만지자 그녀의 가슴은
연민으로 가득 차 하늘로 두둥실 떠오르고

While a man,
a perfect image of a bridegroom
stands at the doorstep.

신랑과 꼭 닮은
남자가 문간에 서 있다

Chuseok

When I leave my homeland, it is late summer; during the days of
Chuseok, a national holiday, the Korean Thanksgiving.

When I am reminded of the old days,
I think of the full moon rising above the hills of my hometown.

Smiling alone while in a small park I fall into memories of Chuseok
Eve;
in the cobalt sky the full moon is always smiling for us.

My friends and I make a campfire, sing a folk song together;
We form a ring and the girls dance *Ganggangsulae.*

Swaying hand in hand, spinning right to left, or opposite,
singing the chorus merrily.

At midnight we eat *Songpyeon,*
rice cakes stuffed with chestnuts and sesame, and topped with honey.

I open my eyes and walk across the village square.
A pedestrian holding a bouquet of pale violet lilacs,
and I think of the coming full moon days.

추석

내가 늦여름에 고국을 떠나는데
추석은 고국의 추수감사절로
국정공휴일이다

옛날을 회상하면 고향의 산 위로
떠오르던 보름달이 생각난다

작은 공원에서 옛 추석 전날 밤을
생각하며 혼자 웃음 짓는다
코발트 빛 하늘에 떠있는 둥근 달은
우리를 보고 항상 웃어준다

친구들과 나는 모닥불을
피워 놓고 노래를 부른다
동그란 원을 만들고 여자들은
강강술래를 한다

손에 손을 잡고 오른쪽 왼쪽
반대쪽으로 돌면서 즐겁게 합창을 한다

자정 무렵에는 밤과 참깨로 속을 넣은
송편을 꿀에 찍어 먹는다

눈을 떠 마을광장으로 가니 보행자 한 사람이
연보라색 라일락 부케를 들고 있다
나는 앞으로 다가올 보름달 뜨는 날들을 생각한다

Hometowns Are Passing

Through the windows of the airplane our hometowns are passing away:
The school buildings with their wide grounds,
and the high belfry of the church,
the spacious golden autumn field,
the mounds and hills and even mountain ranges,
together with a river, are moving farther away.

Suddenly memories of my childhood appear out of the passing.
Like watching a movie backward I see:
a one-room house with a thatched roof in the country,
six children sleeping in one room that has no bed,
father on the right side and mother on the left,
only one blanket between us.

In that small and narrow space I dreamt I was a bird flying free.
Now, on a plane leaving my hometown,
even if the panorama on the ground below disappears
these childhood memories do not leave me.

고향이 지나간다

비행기 창문을 통해 내 고향이 지나간다
넓은 운동장의 학교건물 높은 종탑의 교회
넓은 가을 황금 벌판 언덕과 산들이
강과 함께 먼 곳으로 움직여간다

갑자기 유년시절이 생각난다
시골 초가집 침대도 없는 단칸방에서
이불 한 채만 덮고 아버지는
오른쪽 어머니는 왼쪽
여섯 아이가 함께 자는 걸
영화를 뒤로 돌려보듯 본다

그 작고 좁은 공간에서 나는
새처럼 자유롭게 나는 꿈을 꾸었다
지금 비행기를 타고 고향을 떠나가니
지상의 전경은 멀리 사라지고 있지만
나의 유년의 추억은 사라지지 않는다

Kimchi

Although memories of my hometown are increasingly forgotten,
my favorite Korean food is still in my heart.
How I crave Kimchi!

I cannot forget its characteristic smell—its scallions, ginger and garlic.

The old days are dim, but the longing for this taste continues;
fresh Kimchi on a picnic, fermented Kimchi after a long journey,
mellow-radish Kimchi late at night when the snow is blowing.

In pouring rain or heavy snow I used to drive long distances for Kimchi.

Now I sit under the lamplight with a grey-haired childhood chum.
In the dusk of early evening we watch the full moon rise over the mountain.
Old days have gone by, but my taste for Kimchi is with me, like an old friend.

김치

고향에 대한 기억은 점차 잊혀져 가도
내가 가장 좋아하는 음식 김치는
잊을 수 없다 김치를 향한 나의 갈망!

부추, 생강과 마늘이 함께 만들어내는
독특한 김치냄새를 잊을 수 없다

옛날에 대한 기억은 희미해져 가도
소풍 갔을 때 먹었던 겉절이 김치 맛
긴 여행 후 먹었던 발효 김치 맛, 눈 오는 날
먹었던 잘 익은 무김치 맛은 잊을 수 없다

비가 퍼붓거나 눈이 펑펑 내려도
나는 김치 때문에 먼 길을 가곤 했다

땅거미 지는 초저녁 등불 아래
반백의 유년친구와 함께
산 위로 떠오르는 둥근 달을 바라본다
옛날은 갔어도 김치에 대한 취향은
나와 나의 친구에게 변함없이 남아있다

Hammer and Sickle

The scars on my left fingers remind me of my childhood.
During the Korean War we were poor and miserable.
Hungry, I wandered the streets to find food.

Sometimes, even though I was a very young boy, I worked at construction sites,
using a hammer to break stones into small pieces for the concrete bridges.

Sometimes I was careless and the hammer hit my finger.
Each time the wounds took longer to heal.

In summer I went out to the fields to cut fodder for compost,
mowing grass with a sickle and repeatedly injuring my fingers.

The hammer and sickle were my familiar childhood friends,
teaching me the sanctity of bread, rest and freedom.

망치와 낫

나의 왼손가락을 보면 유년시절이 생각난다
전쟁 중 우리는 가난하고 비참했다
배가 고파 먹을 것을 찾아 거리를 헤맸다

아주 어린 나이에 때로는 공사장에서
콘크리트 다리를 만드는데 쓰려고
망치로 돌을 잘게 깨는 일을 했다

그 일을 하다가 때때로 손가락을
망치로 때리는 실수를 해 부상을 당했고
그때마다 치유하는 데 시간이 걸렸다

여름에는 들로 나가 퇴비감과 풀을 낫으로
베면서 손가락을 계속 다쳤다

망치와 낫은 나에게 빵과 휴식과 자유의
신성함을 가르쳐준 유년의 친구다

Too Late

In late spring she called, asking me softly, with kindness in her voice,
"Come to my home to play before the cherry blossoms fall."
"I'll try my best," I said, but never went after all.

Even forgetting her name for a long time after.

One dark winter night I visit with a white chrysanthemum.
While driving to her, Beethoven's Symphony No.5 flows from the car radio,
petals from the chrysanthemum and seeds of balsam flowers
pour out onto the seat.

The seeds seem to breathe, the buds rise,
and soon the red-colored flowers bloom clearly;
I dye her fingernails with the petals of garden balsams,
then her face is wreathed in smile.

In spite of myself, days come and go quickly.

Many friends and acquaintances attend the send-off ceremony of her spirit.
In front of her portrait there is a black rosary and many flowers.
I place a white chrysanthemum before her.

너무 늦었어요

늦봄에 그녀는 내게 전화로
"벚꽃 지기 전에 우리 집에 놀러 와" 라고 해서
내가 "최선을 다 해볼게" 라고 대답했지만
결국에는 가지 않았다

그 후 오랜 세월
그녀의 이름마저 잊고 살았다

어느 어두운 겨울날 밤 나는 하얀 국화 한 송이를 들고
그녀를 방문한다 차를 운전해 가는 도중 라디오에서
베토벤 5번 교향곡이 흘러나오고 자동차 좌석에
마른 국화 꽃잎과 봉선화 씨가 떨어진다

꽃씨는 숨을 쉬는 듯 싹이 트고 난 후
곧 선명한 붉은 색깔의 꽃을 피운다
내가 그녀의 손톱을 텃밭 봉숭아로
물들여주자 그녀는 환하게 웃는다

나도 모르는 사이
세월은 유수처럼 흐른다

많은 친구와 지인들이 그녀의 영결식에 참석한다
그녀의 초상 앞에는 까만 염주와 많은 꽃들이 놓여있다
나는 하얀 국화 한 송이를 그녀 앞에 놓는다

The Sorrow

I'm at the window with the green tea she sent me.
I'm drinking the leisure hour of the afternoon
contained wholly in the tea
that has brewed little by little.

The sorrow spreads silently like a shadow
and drifts like a wind.
Appearing unexpectedly from time to time
though it never seems to stand in the way of the wide steps of life.

Now it comes together
with the fragrance of the tea.
Then ebbs from me.

Like a mass of dough in the hands of a baker.
Could I knead this sorrow 'till it is pliable?
Or like soft down on a thistle
is it possible for it to blow away completely?

While I drink slowly she is with me silently.
Spreads over the quiet surface of the cup with fragrance
and slips into my heart.

슬픔

나는 창문 가에 서서 그녀가 보내 준 녹차를 마신다
조금씩 우러나는 차 속에 온전히 녹아든
오후의 한가함을 마시고 있다

슬픔은 그림자처럼 소리 없이 번졌다가
바람처럼 사라진다
슬픔은 종종 불시에 나를 찾아온다
그러나 슬픔이 내 인생의 큰 발걸음을
막아설 것 같지는 않다

이제 슬픔은 차의 향기와 함께
내게 왔다 썰물처럼 떠나간다

제빵사 손에 들린 밀가루 반죽처럼 나는
이 슬픔을 주물러 부드럽게 만들 수 있을까
아니면 엉겅퀴의 연모처럼
바람에 날려 없앨 수는 없을까

내가 한가로움을 마시는 동안
그녀는 조용히 내 곁에 머물다
향기로운 찻잔 표면을 거쳐
내 가슴 속으로 성큼 걸어 들어온다

Storyline

In the picture his eyes are smiling as before.
But she still has a heart fraught with sorrow.
It might take more time to leave this love.

First thing in the morning she greets him.
And each day when she leaves for the office
he sees her off from his place in the family room.

When she comes back home she tries not to spend so much time there,
decreasing the length of her conversations with him.
She waits for the day she will forget what might have been fruitful;
but it is not easy.

The smile in the gilt-framed picture contains all of the stories:
that discourse about the operas
that she used to watch with him.

But there is no sound from the photo.
Now he seems to be
keeping silence.

Yet he is still smiling
and her fruit is yet ripe.
Although the framed picture
is covered with dust.

스토리 라인

사진 속 그의 눈은 전처럼 웃고 있지만
그녀의 가슴은 슬픔으로 가득하다
이 사랑을 떠나보내는 데는
더 많은 시간이 걸릴 것 같다

아침에 그녀는 그에게 인사부터 한다
매일 아침 그녀가 출근을 하면
그는 거실에 있는 자신의 자리에서
그녀를 배웅한다

그녀가 퇴근하면 그와 많은 시간을 보내지 않고
함께 대화하는 시간도 줄인다
그녀는 아쉬운 지난날들을 잊으려 하지만
그게 쉽지 않다

금박 액자 속 그의 미소는 그녀가 그와 함께
보곤 했던 오페라의 줄거리를 말해주지만

사진에 있는 그는 아무 소리 없이
침묵만 지키고 있다

그래도 그는 아직 웃고 있다
그녀의 과일은 아직 무르익어 있는데
액자 속 사진에는 먼지만 쌓이고 있다

Seollal

The Lunar New Year's Day, Seollal, always brings nostalgia;
sometimes I return to my hometown in Korea.
We were poor, but happy together
and always had a good time during Seollal.

Sometimes we eat *Tteokuk*, Korea's traditional Sliced Rice Cake Soup,
or wear *Hanbok*, Korea's traditional dress, and visit friends and relatives.
The children bow to the adults and receive their cash gifts,
and play *Yutnori*, a customary board game;
usually I am disqualified but not displeased.

Sometimes I visit our ancestors' graves to pay my respects to them,
and to the old places with the children to learn our history.
Sometimes, in the winter season I ski
while coming down along the ridge of the mountain
or sleigh ride along the freezing river.
Some winter seasons great flakes of snow continue falling day and night
for several days, and then the whole town is buried.

Now, in San Francisco, I get out of my car for a walk alone on Seollal
and I stand on a trail in the hills at dusk.
A boy is flying a colorful kite
and the western skies are lit up with the glow of the setting sun.

The red tail of the kite flickers in the soft breeze
It seems to beckon me to follow.
Suddenly memories of childhood come back in rapid succession,
like the rising tide.

I send greetings to my homeland
through the kite's string that might be extended there.

설날

설날, 음력 정월 초하룻날에는 항상 향수에 젖는다
그래서 때로는 코리아에 있는 고향을 방문하기도 한다
우리는 가난했지만 함께 행복했고
설날에는 항상 즐거운 시간을 보냈다

때로는 가래떡을 잘게 썰어 국을 끓인 떡국을 먹고
코리아의 전통 옷 한복을 입고 친지들을 찾는다
아이들은 어른들에게 절을 하고 세뱃돈을 받고
전통 윷놀이를 한다 나는 자주 중도탈락 되지만
기분 나쁘지 않다

선산에 성묘도 하고 아이들과 유적을 찾아 역사
공부도하고 산등성이서 겨울스키를 타기도하고
꽁꽁 언 강에서 썰매를 타기도 한다
어떤 겨울에는 밤낮으로 함박눈이 며칠 동안
펑펑 내려 마을전체가 눈에 파묻히기도 한다

이제 샌프란시스코에서 맞은 설날 나 홀로
차에서 내려 황혼이 지는 산길을 오른다
석양이 붉게 타는 서편하늘을 배경으로
한 소년이 화려한 연을 날리고 있다

연의 붉은 꼬리가 미풍에 깜박거려 마치
나에게 따라오라고 손짓을 하는 것 같다
이윽고 유년의 추억들이 밀물처럼 밀려온다

나는 고국까지 뻗어 있을 법한 연줄을 통해
고국에다 안부를 전한다

Under the Old Pine

I read my friend's letter under the old pine tree—it's similar to the pine at home
that looks like a big mushroom or huge umbrella to shelter me.
The trunk of the tree shows the motion of time, but its needles remain green.

The pine tree standing regally in the backwoods of my hometown
was the guardian of our neighborhood. As a young boy, I played hide-and-seek
with my childhood friends around the pine tree and dreamed my dreams.

Now I stand, leaning back on the trunk of the old pine tree in
New York's Central Park.
Homesick for those days, I play the harmonica to relieve nostalgia, sing a folk
song continuously, and call my childhood friend's name repeatedly.

Under the old pine tree
I write a letter to my dear friend.
And a pleasant childhood day comes back to me.

Now what do I gain from my labor at which I toil here?
While I didn't notice that the sun rose and set, then hurried back to where
it rose again, my hair has been turning grey.

All things are like the clouds in the sky that appear for awhile and vanish.
Like chasing after wind,
nothing is gained here.

This winter may also pass soon
and the spring disappear;
the summer too will vanish and then this year.

I'd like to gather up my things and
head back to my hometown.
What do I gain from my labor at which I toil here?

While writing my letter
the full moon rises far away above the horizon.
The same moon my friend may also see under the old tree there.

노송 아래서

큰 버섯과 우산 모양의 고향 소나무를 닮은
노송 아래서 친구의 편지를 읽는다
소나무 몸통은 연륜을 말해주고 잎은 푸르다

고향 뒷산의 위풍당당한 소나무는 우리 동네 수호신이었다
어린 시절 나는 친구들과 함께 소나무 근처에서
숨바꼭질을 하면서 꿈을 키웠다

이제 나는 뉴욕 센트럴파크의 노송에 기대어
어린 시절을 그리워하며 향수를 달래 보려고
하모니카를 불고 민요도 부르면서
유년친구들의 이름을 자꾸만 불러본다

노송아래서 친구에게 편지를 쓰니
즐거웠던 유년의 추억이 떠오른다

나는 여기에서 힘들게 일하며 무엇을 얻고 있나
해가 떴다 지고 떴던 곳으로 서둘러 되돌아가는 걸
미처 보지도 못하는 동안에 머리는 반백이 됐구나

모든 것이 잠시 하늘에 생겨났다 사라지는 구름 같고
바람을 쫓는 것 같아 여기서 얻을 게 하나도 없네

이 겨울도 곧 지나가고 봄도 여름도 다 지나가고
결국에는 올해도 다 가겠지

짐을 챙겨 고향으로 돌아가리라
여기서 힘들게 일하며 얻는 게 무엇인가

편지를 쓰는 동안 수평선 멀리 둥근 달이 떠오른다
저 달을 내 친구도 고향의 노송 아래서 볼지도 몰라

Light and Shadow

Her brown hair flutters in the gentle breeze.
Shining in the sunlight—dancing a dance of the zephyr.

She sleeps on her fiancé's shoulder.
Her mouth open
as if she is singing a solo.

Tangled hair, no makeup, no lipstick
her breasts exposed.

In this manner, ugliness is exchanged for beauty—
the intelligence of her fiancé for her own shortcomings.
Her dreams are hers but outside of her.

Light pours in through the crevices of the clouds,
scurries across her.
Then the shadow of a cloud.

But it doesn't concern her
that the light and shadow come and go
while she sleeps.

Or that the weather will cycle clear and cloudy
at irregular intervals.
Or that their abiding hour is fleeting.

빛과 그림자

빛나는 그녀의 갈색 머리칼이 미풍 속에
춤추듯 나부낀다

그녀는 혼자 노래를 부르듯 입을 벌리고
약혼자의 어깨를 베고 잠을 잔다

흐트러진 머리에 화장도 않고 립스틱도
바르지 않은 얼굴에 가슴을 드러내고 있다

이렇게 그녀의 추함은 아름다움으로
그녀의 단점은 약혼자의 지성으로 대체된다
그녀의 꿈은 그녀 것이지만 그녀 밖에 있다

구름의 틈새로 쏟아지는 햇빛이 그녀를 스쳐
지나가고 난 후 구름이 그림자를 드리운다

그녀가 잠들어 있는 동안 빛이 나든 그림자가 지든
날씨가 불규칙적 간격으로 맑아지든 흐려지든
날씨가 금방 변하든 말든 그녀가 알 바 아니다

Faded Letter

While putting my desk in order
I stumbled across a faded letter.

It seemed I wrote it a long time ago,
but now I no longer understand the words.

Vestiges of adolescence hang in the sky;
as a young yellow-colored butterfly.

I had painted a rainbow-colored dream on paper
and was delighted with you.

But even now you are bringing me flowers.
A floral perfume
that emanates from the drawings.

Like a hieroglyphic letter from ancient people
this becomes a legendary story.

At the moment I put the letter into the drawer
I see a butterfly float aimlessly away
outside my window.

빛 바랜 편지

책상을 정리하다가
빛 바랜 편지를 본다

오래전 쓴 편지 같은데
읽어봐도 무슨 소린지 알 수 없다

사춘기의 자취가
앳된 노랑나비처럼 하늘에 걸려있다

나는 무지갯빛 꿈을 종이에 그려 넣고
그대와 함께 기뻐했다

그러나 그대는 지금도 내게 꽃을 가져온다
그림에서 뿜어져 나오는 꽃 향기

고대인들이 보내온 상형문자 편지처럼
이것은 전설이 된다

내가 서랍에 편지를 넣는 순간
나는 나비 한 마리가 창문 밖으로
표연히 흘러가는 걸 본다

White Porcelain Vase

On a small table in the corner of a Buddhist altar
sits a white porcelain vase.
How long has it been there I wonder?

The moonlight flows together with a stream
in the black and white painting.
Two carps meet where the gentle waves
approach the side of the frame.

The warm sunshine enters the room
through the windows covered with Oriental paper.
The sunshine brightens the room and the full moon in the painting.
From another room, a wooden gong sounded by a priest is heard faintly.

The bell permeates the empty void
softly filling the room fully.
Pushes me to renounce my mundane agonies
and flow along with the stream in the painting
of the antique white porcelain vase.

After awhile the windows are opened slightly.
Outside the dried leaves are scattered on the ground
by the brisk wind.

백자

불단 구석 작은 탁자 위에
백자 한 개가 외롭게 놓여있다
백자는 그곳에 얼마 동안 놓여있는 것일까

달빛이 흑백 그림 속의 냇물과 함께 흐른다
그림 속에는 부드러운 물결이 한쪽으로 흘러가고
두 마리의 잉어가 그곳에서 만나고 있다

한지로 만든 창문을 통해
따스한 햇볕이 들어온다
햇볕은 방과 그림 속의 둥근 달을 비춰준다
다른 방에서 스님의 목탁 소리가 들려온다

종소리가 빈 공간으로 스며들어
방안을 가득 채우며
나에게 세속의 고뇌를 버리고
골동백자에 그려진 냇물을 따라
흘러가라고 종용한다

잠시 후 창문이 조금 열리니
밖에는 마른 잎이 세찬 바람에
떨어져 땅에 뒹굴고 있다

Bronze Image of Buddha

On an open corner
at the Asian Art Museum in San Francisco,
a bronze Buddha is attentively listening, despite a crowd of visitors.

He doesn't care about me. Yet I approach him.
Up close I see that his ears are open to the outside:
the clamor made by men and women, the earth, sky, clouds, and wind…
all things in Nature.

Finally, after a long time
these reverberations mingle together
and are heard simply as one sound.

The Buddha's dark-gray complexion shows me an eternity.
He seems to laugh at me,
enduring this waiting, endeavoring to be humble.

With eyes slightly open and grasping another's hand in front,
He is endlessly and eagerly listening,
seeking the noise from outside.

I close my eyes and calmly review days past.

부처님 청동상

샌프란시스코 아시아 예술박물관의
개방된 한쪽 코너에 있는 부처님 동상은
수많은 방문객들이 찾아와도 정중하게 귀를 기울인다

부처님은 내게 관심이 없지만
나는 부처님께 가까이 다가간다
가까이서 보니 부처님 귀가 밖으로 열려 있다
남자와 여자 하늘과 땅 바람과 구름 등
자연의 모든 것을 향해 열려 있다

한참 후 마지막에는 이 모든 반향들이
뒤섞여 오직 한 가지
소리로만 들린다

짙은 회색의 부처님 안색은 영원의 세계를 보여준다
부처님은 겸허해지길 애쓰시며
기다림의 시간을 참아내며 나를 보고 웃으시는 것 같다

부처님은 눈을 가늘게 뜨고 앞에 있는
다른 사람의 손을 잡고 밖에서 들려오는
시끄러운 소리에도 신경을 쓰면서
끝없이 열심히 듣고 계신다

나는 눈을 감고 조용히
지난날들을 돌이켜본다

For the Chrysanthemum

When other flowers fall in autumn she blooms alone.

Despite frosty mornings,
her work is to become glorious petals.
And the air is laden with the scent of chrysanthemums.

In order to come into bloom
the chrysanthemum endures
scorching heat that confines her for days in summer.

She hears rolls of thunder in the distance
and feels heavy showers falling whole days.

She sees flocks of swans fly away through dark clouds before sunset.
She is cultivated from gentle breezes in the mountains.

In her short life, the chrysanthemum has experienced prosperity and adversity.
Once the chrysanthemums are fallen, no other flowers remain.

I pray to God, I wish not to follow her too soon
into the dark and cold winter night.

국화를 위하여

가을에 다른 꽃들이 질 때
국화는 홀로 핀다

추운 아침에도 국화는
눈부시게 아름다운 꽃잎을 피우고
대기를 국화꽃 향기로 채운다

국화는 꽃잎을 피우기 위하여
여름의 무더운 날들을 꼼짝도
하지 않고 견뎌낸다

국화는 멀리서 나는 천둥소리를 듣고
온종일 굵은 소낙비를 맞는다

국화는 해지기 전 검은 구름 사이로
백조 떼가 날아가는 걸 보며
산속의 부드러운 산들바람 속에서 자란다

짧은 일생동안 국화는
쓴맛 단맛을 모두 경험한다
국화가 지고 나면 어떤 다른 꽃도 남아있지 않다

나는 국화를 따라 너무 일찍 어둡고
추운 밤에 들지 않기를 기도한다

Unknown Flowers in the Valley

The flowers bloom.
The flowers bloom.
The unknown flowers bloom
in the valleys of the mountain
from spring to summer.

Because of loving the silence,
the flowers bloom alone.
The flowers bloom lonely
among the weeds
in the secluded valleys.

Because of loving the sun,
the flowers bloom from day to day.
The unknown flowers bloom
from day to day continually.

Because of not wanting
to show their shabby leaves,
the flowers fade away in the evening.
The flowers fade away together with the wind.
The unknown flowers vanish away silently.

계곡의 이름 모를 꽃

꽃이 핀다
꽃이 핀다
산속 계곡에서 봄부터 가을까지
이름 모를 꽃이 핀다

적막을 사랑하기에
꽃은 홀로 핀다
외딴 계곡 잡초 속에서
외로이 핀다

꽃은 태양을 사랑하기에
날이면 날마다 핀다
이름 모를 꽃이
날이면 날마다 끊임없이 핀다

초라한 잎을 보여주고 싶지 않아
꽃은 저녁에 진다
꽃은 바람과 함께 진다
이름 모를 꽃은
조용히 사라진다

While Sweeping the Leaves in My Back Yard

In autumn I sweep the leaves every day.
There are many kinds of deciduous trees
older than neighboring evergreens.

In spring, these trees come into leaf at different times,
but descend in autumn simultaneously
after the color has faded.

In summer, the leaves grow luxuriantly
taking various shapes that cast shadows
that block the glaring sunlight at noon
and call up mysterious forest spirits and creatures
on a windy evening.

In frosty autumn, once upright and prosperous leaves
hang their browning heads down.
The fallen leaves lie down together in the recesses,
living together peacefully.

I sweep the leaves together.
Assembling them into piles outside my yard.
To be taken away by the garbage truck in the morning.

뒤뜰에서 낙엽을 쓸며

가을에는 나는 매일 낙엽을 쓴다
근처의 상록수보다 더 오래된
여러 종류의 낙엽수들이 있다

이 나무들은 봄에 시차를 두고 잎이 돋지만
가을에 단풍이 들어
질 때는 한꺼번에 진다

여름에 나뭇잎들은 여러 가지 모습으로
풍성하게 자라나 대낮이면 눈부신 햇빛을
차단해주는 그늘을 만들고 바람 부는 저녁이면
신비스러운 숲의 요정들과 동물들을 불러온다

차가운 가을이 오면 한때 반듯하고 풍요롭던
잎들은 갈색으로 변한 머리를 아래로 내려뜨린다
낙엽들은 웅덩이에 함께 평화롭게 누워있다

낙엽들을 한꺼번에 쓸어 모아
마당 밖에 쌓아 두면
아침에 청소차가 실어간다

Growth Ring

In the front yard of my house
stand several large maples.
Taller than all the others
in the neighborhood.

As soon as they appear ready to bud in spring
I take notice.
Watch intently each day as the leaves grow luxuriantly.
Finally forming a dense, gloomy thicket in summer.

My windows look out into the garden, and
even though I take tea every day
seeing the same trees outside
I do not anticipate them turning with autumn's color.

Many squirrels live in these trees.
Spending their time scurrying up and down.
Once one, while going down, suddenly stopped
to look at me, his eyes meeting mine.

After a meal in the dining room
I climb the stairs to my second floor study,
and a squirrel also goes up to the top,
by way of the trunk of the tree.

The maple leaves, now brown, have fallen.
In such a short time the trees have become scrawny.

When evening falls all things
are covered with darkness.
Another morning is preparing to be opened.
Each day is just like every other day.

The squirrels and I travel up and down
and the tree's growth ring increases annually.

나이테

내 집 앞마당에는
이웃의 다른 나무들보다 키가 큰
단풍나무가 몇 그루 심어져 있다

봄에 싹이 틀 기미가 보일 때부터
잎이 무성하게 자라 여름에 짙고
음침한 숲으로 변하는 날까지
매일처럼 면밀히 관찰한다

창문이 정원 쪽으로 열려 있어
매일같이 차를 마시며 창밖에 있는
나무들을 바라보지만 그것들이 가을에 단풍이
들 것이라는 생각은 미처 하지 못하고 바라본다

이 나무들에는 다람쥐가 여러 마리 살고 있어
나무를 오르락내리락 한다
한번은 다람쥐 한 마리가 나무에서 내려오다
갑자기 멈추더니 나와 눈이 마주쳤다

식당에서 저녁을 먹고 이층에 있는
서재로 올라가니 다람쥐도
나무를 타고 올라간다

이제 갈색으로 변한 나뭇잎은 모두 떨어지고
단풍나무들은 이렇게 며칠 만에 앙상해졌다

저녁이 되자 만물은 어둠에 휩싸인다
새로운 아침이 문을 열 준비를 한다
똑같은 날이 매일 반복된다

다람쥐와 나는 위아래로 왔다 갔다 하고
나무의 나이테는 해마다 늘어간다

The Last Leaf of Autumn

All, all are left but one;
the last lonely leaf swaying in cold winds.

Showing her silvery underside;
destined to come down soon.

All her lovely companions
have faded away.

The branches of the trees are thin—
their leaves all vanished.

Hour by hour it grows colder.
Just before sunset the clouds drop down.

Like the leaf,
I almost fall fluttering in the wind.

Like the leaf, I nearly fall fluttering from
the branches of myself.

In days past I missed out on something spiritual.
And I wasted time and effort.

If I were a balmy breeze I'd talk with her.
If I were a swift cloud I'd fly to former days.

I will not leave her to waste on the branch.
All will join me in singing her praises.

가을의 마지막 잎

낙엽은 모두 떨어지고
오직 한 개 낙엽만이 바람에 흔들리고 있다

낙엽의 안쪽은 은빛
곧 떨어질 수밖에 없는 운명이다

사랑스러운 동료들은
모두 사라졌다

나뭇가지들은 가늘어졌고
나뭇잎들은 모두 사라졌다

시시각각으로 날은 추워진다
일몰 직전에 구름은 사라졌다

나뭇잎처럼
나도 흔들리며 떨어질 것 같다

나뭇잎처럼 나도 나 자신이라는
나뭇가지에서 흔들려 떨어질 것 같다

전에는 일종의 정신적 상실감으로 인해
시간과 노력을 낭비하였다

내가 훈훈한 산들바람이라면
저 마지막 잎과 대화할 수 있을 텐데
내가 재빠른 구름이라면
지난날로 날아가 볼 수 있을 텐데

나는 저 마지막 잎이 나뭇가지에서
헛되이 사라지게 하지 않을 것이다
남들도 모두 나처럼
저 마지막 잎을 찬양할 것이다

Ripened Pumpkin

Loose and abundant woman.
Woman of lenient mind
lying on the sofa.

She offers comfort
and humor
I rest in her sunny smile.

Innocent, round, nude.
Fattened from soil
and earth.

익은 호박

헐겁고 풍만한 여인
관대한 마음씨의 여인이
소파에 누워있다

그녀는 나를 위로하고
유머로 나를 즐겁게 한다
나는 그녀의 빛나는 미소 속에
휴식을 취한다

흙과 땅에서 살을 찌운
순진하고 동그란
발가벗은 여인

The Heavy Snow, The Chaos

I

All day, every day, the snow is falling ceaselessly;
Until all things on the earth are covered with snow.
And due to severe
descending
snow
visibility is nearly zero.
It seems that a piece of the heavens has quietly opened,
failing to control the quantities of snow falling to earth.
Or perhaps after being scolded by the heavens
the clouds work off their vexations with heavy snowfall…
Like a master kicking a dog who has disobeyed.

II

At the first snow day, the yards and roads were slightly covered
with light and soft snowflakes.
Everything was rounded off, smoothed over, magnificently.
However, the next day, the true character of the snowflakes was revealed.
Then they submerged the alleys and cars nearly to their windows,
broke the trees and roofs of barns.
Piled up snow closed the doors of houses and stores.
Now confines all citizens to their homes.
The city was put out of commission by the snow.

III

The snow, although trampled and humbled,
still behaves perversely.

대설과 혼란

I

매일 온종일 눈이 쉬지 않고 내린다
세상 만물이 눈에 덮일 때까지 내린다
내리는 함박눈 때문에 눈앞이 거의 보이지 않는다
하늘 한 부분이 소리 없이 열려
대지로 내리는 눈의 양을
조절하지 못하고 있는 것 같다
아니면 하늘에서 야단을 맞은 구름이
마치 개 주인이 말 안 듣는 개를 걷어차듯이
함박눈을 가지고서 화풀이를 하는 것 같다

II

눈이 처음 오는 날 눈송이는 마당과 길을 얇고
부드러운 눈송이로 살짝 덮었다
만물은 눈에 덮여 아름다운 모습으로 변했다
그러나 그 다음날 눈송이는 본연의 모습을 드러냈다
눈송이는 골목길은 물론 차창까지 덮고
헛간의 지붕을 무너뜨렸다
집과 가게의 문은 쌓인 눈으로 인해 닫혀버렸다
이제는 시민들이 모두 집에 갇혀버렸다
도시는 눈으로 인해 기능이 마비되었다

III

눈은 짓밟혀 초라해져도
짓궂은 행동을 하기는 마찬가지다

One Freezing Day

Minus twenty-one degrees Celsius this morning—
The mountains, rivers, lakes, trees, and even myself, are frozen over.

In freezing days such as these
I imagine
descending
into the earth
and living there
together
with roots.

And even though the earth is frozen with ice
and all the grasses are withered,
I will hear the murmuring
of the brooks that flow
through the numerous roots in the ground.
Underground tubers and bulbs preparing
for new life
with the coming spring.

And in the ground beneath
I may be invited by the moles to a New Year's Eve party.
Where warm in their burrow perhaps I will see their folk dances
that I never experienced above ground ...
What genial places there are underground!

I imagine
after the winter season passes
I will return home,
together with the frogs.

어느 추운 날

오늘아침은 섭씨 영하 21도
산과 강 호수와 나무 심지어는
나 자신까지 얼어버렸다

이처럼 추운 날에는
나는 땅속으로 내려가
나무뿌리와 함께 사는 걸 상상한다

대지는 얼고 풀은 모두 시들었지만
나는 땅속의 수많은 나무뿌리 사이로
흐르는 냇물의 속삭임을 듣는다
땅속에서는 덩이줄기와 구근들이
새봄과 함께 새로운 생명을 준비하고 있다

그리고 나는 두더지들의 땅속 송년파티에
초대를 받아 따뜻한 두더지 구멍에서
지상에서는 보지 못했던 두더지
민속춤을 구경할지도 모르겠다

땅속은 얼마나 정감이 가는 곳인가
추운 겨울이 지난 후 나는
개구리들과 함께 귀가하는 걸 상상해 본다

The Day Is Snowing, I'm Comfortably Warm

All morning
slow clouds smoothly flying
over the front
and back yard.

For the last several days
low clouds hanging
in the foreground of the mountains.
Covered with a veil of clouds.

Day and night whole clouds
assemble in the Heavens.
Preparing great snowflakes.
Now falling softly and silently through the bare branches of trees.

It's as if someone operates a magnificent factory in the sky.
Where all kinds of clouds, long shreds and tatters of fog,
the cries of birds, and even the sound of words,
are mixed.

And stripped of color, become
these snowflakes descending to the fields.
Like green sugar cane changed
to white refined sugar in the factories.

The day is snowing, I'm comfortably warm.
Even though the weather is below freezing.
I walk up and down through the hamlet park
humming "White Christmas."

Great snowflakes are falling in the pines.
Making big snowy tassels in the boughs.

From above, the clouds are gazing on the astonishing panorama of our hamlet.
From the clouds, the snowflakes are descending continuously.

And my buoyant mind is ascending to the sky
like a balloon.

눈 내리는 날 느끼는 따스함

앞마당과 뒷마당 위로
구름이 천천히 부드럽게
이동하고 있다

지난 며칠 동안 구름이
산의 앞쪽에 걸려있어
산에 구름 베일을 씌워주고 있다

밤낮을 가리지 않고 구름들이
모두 하늘에 모여 대설을 준비해왔고
지금은 벌거벗은 나뭇가지 사이로
조용하고 부드럽게 눈송이를 뿌리고 있다

여러 가지 구름과 길고 작은 안개조각과
새의 울음소리와 심지어는 사람의
말소리까지 뒤섞는 공장을 누군가가
하늘에서 운영하고 있는 것 같다

초록빛 사탕수수가 공장에서 정제되어
하얀색의 설탕으로 바뀌듯
눈송이들은 자신의 색깔을 잃고
들판에 내린다

눈이 내리는 날이지만 나는 따스함을 느낀다
날씨는 영하로 춥지만 나는 "화이트 크리스마스"를
흥얼거리며 마을 공원을 거닌다

커다란 눈송이들이 소나무 위로 내려
나뭇가지에다 큼지막한 장식을 한다

구름이 뒤에서 우리 마을의
놀랄만한 전경을 바라보고 있다
구름은 눈송이를 쉬지 않고 뿌려 댄다

그리고 나의 들뜬 마음은
풍선처럼 하늘로 날아오른다

A Snowman Smiled

In the calm and emptiness of the hamlet park
a sturdy lad stands alone in front of a tall pine.
He is a horrid and ridiculous figure.

His left arm is broken.
One large eye made with charcoal and deep-black eyebrows almost gone.
A mustache made with pine needles is cut in half.
Only traces of a nose and mouth remain.

In his right hand he tightly holds an American flag,
like a soldier wounded in many battles.

I feel pity for him.

I restore his arm, eyes, eyebrows, mustache, nose and mouth.
Then after reinforcing the face and body with snowflakes,
I cover his neck with a red muffler.

I think he will be happy and smile at last.
But still he looks wooden, expressionless, lonely.
So I make another snowman exactly the same beside him.

And as I turn to head toward home
I hear a deep laughing voice at my back.

눈사람이 웃었다

조용하고 텅 빈 마을공원에 건장한 청년이
커다란 소나무 앞에 혼자 서 있다
그의 모습은 흉하고 우스꽝스럽다

왼팔은 부러졌고 눈 한 개는
커다란 숲으로 만들어진 짙고 검은 눈썹은
거의 다 없어졌다 솔잎으로 만든 콧수염은
반이 잘려 나갔고 코와 입은 있던 흔적만 남아있다

그는 여러 전투를 거쳐 부상당한
군인처럼 오른손에 미국 국기를 들고 있다

나는 그에게 연민을 느낀다

나는 그의 팔과 눈과 눈썹과 콧수염과
코와 입을 다시 만들어준다
그리고는 얼굴과 몸을 눈송이로 보강해주고
목에는 빨간 목도리를 해주었다

나는 그가 마침내 행복한 웃음을 지을 거라 생각하지만
그는 아직도 딱딱하고 무표정하고 외롭다
그래서 나는 그와 똑같은 눈사람을 만들어
그 옆에 세워 놓는다

그런 후 내가 집으로 향해 발걸음을 옮길 때
나는 그가 굵고 낮게 웃는 소리를 듣는다

Into The Snowy Field

When he entered the university from Korea
he had no spare clothes.
Wearing dark blue jeans the first day,
and every day, until he graduated.

His classmates thought he had an obsession for jeans.
But he confided in me
that once in a while he would have liked to have worn leather pants,
a jacket with a fur lining.

After we spoke
he walked across the campus
into the field
toward the horizon
with big flakes of snow falling
as they had for several days.

After graduation we scattered.
Each to survive on our own,
out in the vast field of the world.

I saw his portrait in the paper,
set out with a border of white chrysanthemums.
I read about the car accident on the highway during a snowy winter day.

In the photo, he was wearing blue jeans.
Who else but I knew?
How he wished to wear the warmth of leather in cold weather.

눈발으로

그가 코리아에서 와서 대학에 다닐 때
그는 여벌로 입는 옷이 없었다
그래서 입학 첫날부터 대학 졸업할 때까지
매일 다크블루 재킷만 입고 다녔다

동창생들은 그가 재킷에
집착한다고 생각했다
그러나 그는 안쪽에 털 달린 가죽 재킷과 바지를
입고 싶을 때가 있었다고 내게 털어놓았다

우리가 대화를 나눈 후 그는 며칠 동안이나
내리던 함박눈을 맞으며 캠퍼스를 가로질러
지평선을 향해 들판으로 걸어 나갔다

대학 졸업 후 우리는
각자 살 길을 찾아 헤어졌다

나는 신문에서 하얀 국화로 테두리가 장식된
그의 초상화를 보았다
눈 오는 겨울날 고속도로에서 난
교통사고에 관한 기사를 읽었다

영정사진 속에서 그는 다크블루 재킷을 입고 있었다
내가 아니면 누가 알까
그가 얼마나 추운 겨울날씨에
따뜻한 가죽옷을 입고 싶어 했는지를

Fish Sleep

The fish in the Chinese supermarket stare up at the customers.
While the salesman touts their stellar attributes, fish eyes glare.

The fish on the grill stare up at the cook.
Out of the burning fire their eyes glower.

Like singers their mouths are fully opened,
but without the blinking eyes of chorus members.

When they were caught by the fisherman's casting net
they strongly refused; opening their mouth to feed one last time.
As the air tightened around the fish gills…as death approached finally.

The fire burns the fish, eyes still wide open.
Eyes that have no eyelids.
Eyes that neither sleep nor death can close.

When fish sleep the wide Pacific lays a blanket over them.
The sea sings a lullaby to sleep.

While the fish burn on the grill, no one listens.
But the fish mouths are still wide open.

As if they had all joined in singing
the blue waves of the sea.

고기의 잠

중국인 슈퍼마켓에 있는 고기가
고객들을 쳐다본다
판매원이 우수한 품질을 자랑하자 고기는 눈을 부릅뜬다

석쇠 위에 놓인 고기가 요리사를 쳐다본다
타는 불속에서 고기들은 요리사를 노려본다

노래하는 가수들처럼 그들의 입은 딱 벌어지지만
눈을 깜빡 거리는 합창단원들은 없다

고기들이 어부가 던진 그물에 잡혔을 때
그들은 힘차게 저항했다
마지막으로 한 번 더 숨 쉬려 입을 벌리면서
아가미에 숨이 막힐 때 고기에게는 죽음이 임박했다

불은 고기를 태우지만
고기의 눈은 아직 크게 떠 있다
눈썹이 없는 고기의 눈
잠도 죽음도 감게 할 수 없는 고기의 눈

고기들이 잠이 들면 광활한 태평양은
넓은 이불을 고기들에게 덮어준다.
바다는 고기들에게 자장가를 불러준다

고기들이 석쇠 위에서 타는 동안
누구도 타는 소리를 들어주지 않지만
그럼에도 불구하고 고기들의 입은
크게 벌어져 있다

마치 바다의 푸른 파도를 그리는
노래를 합창하는 것처럼

Ice Trout Fishing

There is a tense moment
felt between what's above the ice and what's below.
Only the fishing line serves as an intermediary.

Dim and far from man's reach,
in the deep part of the lake where trout live.
Where hunger stares him in the face.

While keeping quiet beneath thick ice;
always anxious about news on the surface.
What goes on there?

In a slight tent the fisherman spends three days.
Bores a small hole through the ice.
Drops the fishing line with night crawlers on an angler's hook.
Still no biting signal.

Below,
the trout keep their full attention on the delicious smelling bait.
Ecstasy and uncertainty—their appetite, leading them into temptation.

Above,
strong cold ennui for the fisherman.
A parallel tension between trout and man.

얼음 위 송어낚시

얼음 위와 아래 사이에서
긴장이 느껴지는 순간이 있다
단지 낚싯줄만이 중재자 역할을 한다

사람 발길이 닿진 않는 어둑한 곳
송어가 사는 호수의 깊은 곳
그곳에서 송어는 배고픔을 겪고 있다

두꺼운 얼음 밑에서
얼음 위에는
무슨 일이 있을까 항상 궁금해한다

작은 텐트에서 낚시꾼은 사흘을 보낸다
얼음에 작은 구멍을 뚫고 큰 지렁이를
낚시에 꿰어 달은 낚싯줄을 구멍으로 집어넣는다
아직 입질하는 기미가 없다

얼음 밑에서는
송어가 맛있는 냄새가 나는 미끼를 계속 주시하고 있다
황홀감과 불안-그들의 식욕이 유혹을 한다

얼음 위에서는
춥고 강렬한 권태가 낚시꾼을 괴롭힌다
송어와 사람 사이의 긴장감이 평행선을 달린다

View of the Thawing

Thawing snow runny like rice gruel.
As the poor city streets
regain their original appearance.

Boarded up houses, decrepit from lack of care, show their fatigue.
The leaking roofs repaired with plastic sheets
to protect them from relentless rain.

Sidewalks, forcibly awakened from slumber,
now exposed to a medley of noises from cars, children, loudspeakers.
Sidewalks, previously embedded in snow, revealed.
Heaped with trash and dogs' dung, miscellaneous fluids…

The face of the city, fair-skinned, like an imperial princess.
Thawing, slushy, soppy.
Her snowy makeup rapidly effaced by a spring breeze.

녹는 눈을 바라보며

녹는 눈이 마치 흰죽처럼 흘러내린다
초라해 보였던 도시가
원래의 모습을 되찾는다

관리를 안 해 낡은 판자로 막은 집들은
피로에 지친 모습이다
끈질긴 비를 막으려 플라스틱판으로
수리를 했지만 그래도 지붕이 샌다

보도는 연이어 나는 차와 아이들과
확성기가 내는 소리에 잠에서 억지로 깨어난다
눈에 파묻혔던 보도는 이제 눈이 녹으니
그동안 그 위에 쌓였던 쓰레기와 개의 분뇨와
잡동사니 액체들을 드러내 보인다

눈이 녹으니 황녀처럼 하얀 피부의 얼굴을 가졌던
도시가 축축한 진창이 된다
하얗던 눈의 화장은 봄바람에 급속하게 지워진다

Glasses In Winter

It is minus degrees and cloudy.
It feels like it could snow.

The bus stop at the early commuter hour is teeming
with the salaried workers standing in line.
Waiting—I am one of them.

I get on the Number 7 bus, as I do every morning.
But suddenly my view is blocked entirely.

I flounder at the threshold.
Then, like a blind man
stumble to find a seat.

But there is no way to see.
Until the vapor curtain from the outside is drawn back.

I never expected this invisible enemy.
Hiding in the air, attacking my glasses.
Over the wide differences of temperature and humidity.

겨울 안경

영하에 구름 낀 날씨다
왠지 눈이 내릴 것 같다

이른 통근시간에 버스정거장은
줄을 선 월급생활자들로 붐빈다
나도 그중 한 사람으로 줄을 서 기다린다

나는 매일 아침 7번 버스를 탄다
그런데 버스를 타자마다
갑자기 나의 시야가 차단된다

나는 문턱에서
허둥대다가 장님처럼 넘어져
자리에 앉았다

그러나 안경 바깥의 수증기 막이
지위지기 전까지는 아무것도 볼 수 없었다

온도와 습도가 큰 차이가 나면
공중에 숨어 있다가 갑자기 내 안경을 공격하는
눈에 보이지 않는 적을 나는 미처 몰랐다

Abundant Dreaming Palace

The tinged autumnal leaves build a palace in paradise.
A palace that is full of laughter and music for all eternity.
A place where there is no sickness or death.
These autumnal leaves warm my heart and comfort me.

The hills are ablaze with striking color for one week only.
The palace in paradise is hung in the sky.
There is no admission fee to enter
and everyone is welcome to live here.

In the middle of the autumn season
with its ripening fruits and grains
I would like to live in this dreaming palace
for the duration of the season.

풍요로운 꿈의 궁전

단풍잎들이 낙원에다 궁전을 짓는다
웃음과 음악이 영원히 흘러 넘치는 궁전
질병도 없고 죽음도 없는 궁전
단풍잎들은 내 마음을 따뜻하게 위로해준다

산은 오직 일주일 동안만 찬란한 빛을 내며 불탄다
낙원의 궁전은 하늘에 떠있다
누구라도 무료로 입장할 수 있고
여기와 사는 것도 환영이다

과일과 오곡이 무르익는 중추절이 오면
계절이 끝날 때까지 이 꿈의 궁전에
살고 싶어 진다

IV.

Sunset

A man whose face blushes up to the roots of his hair
is passing beyond the western hill.
Empty-handed, not carry anything.
He is always alone.

Hurrying to pass
as if late for an engagement,
he is counseled by the sparrows and the fawns
to go home early, before darkness.

Often he looks happy
with a broad smile on his face.
On these pleasant days he dyes the whole sky—even the clouds—aglow
while passing over the hill.

But when he is in poor spirits
because of his loneliness
he is not seen
for many days.

Sometimes he puts a lamp on the eastern hill
while passing beyond
and vanishes away to the western side.

저녁노을

빈손에 아무것도 지닌 것 없는 사람이
귀까지 빨개진 얼굴로 서산을 넘는다
그는 항상 외롭다

어두워지기 전에 산을 넘으라는
참새와 새기 사슴의 조언을 들었기에
약속시간에 늦은 사람처럼
갈 길을 서둔다

함박웃음 짓는 그는 종종
행복해 보이기도 한다
산을 넘다가 기쁜 날을 맞으면 그의 웃음은
온 하늘과 구름까지도 환하게 빛나게 한다

그러나 외로움으로
기분이 가라앉을 때면
여러 날 동안 보이지 않는다

때로는 지나는 길에 동편 언덕에다
등불을 놓아도 보지만
곧 서편으로 사라지고 만다

While A Paper Boat Sails

I launch a folded paper boat on the stream
where a brook is murmuring down through waterweeds.

A boat I made simply, with a red mast
and the outer bottom colored sky blue.

I launch the boat into gentle waves,
but after awhile it is shaken by a breeze
and shaded by a drift ofclouds.

Sometimes small fish tease the boat dangerously,
and once a ruby dragonfly landed on the top of the mast
its wings spread out, humming a barely audible song.

So the lonely night comes on.
A myriad of stars rise in the sky
and the waves lull the makeshift boat to safety.

종이배 띄우며

수초를 통과해 졸졸 흐르는 물에
종이배를 띄운다

돛대는 빨간색 배 외부 밑바닥은
하늘색으로 간단하게 만든 종이배

잔잔한 물 위에 띄웠지만
얼마 안 가 미풍에 흔들리고
떠도는 구름에 그늘진다

때로는 작은 물고기들이
위험한 장난을 치기도 하고
빨간 잠자리가 날개를 펴고
들릴 듯 말듯 한 소리를 내며
돛대 끝에 앉아있기도 했다

그 후 외로운 밤이 오니
무수한 별들이 하늘에 뜨고
물결이 잠잠해져 종이배는
안전하게 항해를 한다

Chopsticks

My wife and I sit together in a booth
at the bright and clean Chinese restaurant.
It is the slow hour now.

Several pairs of chopsticks are waiting
for the customers at the table.
Like troops of soldiers lined up to be inspected
they are set out in an orderly way.

A well-educated dieter, I've never hailed them.
Yet they seem to call to me...
"Hey Fatty," I hear them say.
I am anxious to be given a good name as a faithful servant.

Even though these chopsticks have much work to do
they have no grievance against the owner.
They always act in unison.
Not separately.

They do not discriminate by sex or race.
They form a perfectly equitable society of companions.

It is natural that there are keen competitions among men.
But imagine the gains made while cooperating with each other.

Prior to their work,
the chopsticks are resting for awhile together.

젓가락

아내와 나는 밝고 청결한
중국식당 부스에 함께 앉는다
지금은 느긋한 시간이다

젓가락 몇 짝이 식탁에서
손님을 기다리고 있다
검열을 받으려고 도열한
군인들처럼 질서정연하게 놓여있다

다이어트 교육을 잘 받은 나는
그들에게 먼저 인사를 건네지 않는다
그럼에도 그들은 나를 부른다
"뚱보 안녕" 이라는 인사말이 들려온다
나는 신의 있는 친구라는 평판을 얻기를 바란다

이 젓가락들이 많은 일을 하지만
주인에 대해서는 나쁜 감정이 없다
항상 동시에 행동하며 따로 행동하지 않는다

그들은 성이나 인종을 차별하지 않는다
동료들과 함께 완벽하게 공평사회를 구현한다

그들끼리 치열하게 경쟁하는 것은 자연스러운 일이다
그러나 서로 협력하면서 얻는 소득을 생각해보라

일을 시작하기 전 그들은
잠깐 함께 휴식을 취한다

Painting

Sometimes the carelessly lined circle becomes a flower.
And a casually drawn horizontal line becomes the place
where Earth meets up with Heaven.

I glimpse the bony branches while I sketch…
The lines on the paper become the morning sunlight.
Or the thorns of rose bushes.

Bright flowers bloom.

The rose thorns turn into pins which pierce the fin
of the fishes like memories
that are sleeping in the deep lake.

The lilies are shy and smiling,
hiding in the woods.

I'm listening to Vivaldi's "Four Seasons."

Outside, it is raining; gusty winds whip around me.
And lightning strikes with a loud voice.

Just at that moment the electric lights go out.
Everything vanishes into the darkness.
I light a candle and start again—

Put my pencil to the blank page.

그림 그리기

때로는 아무렇게나 그린 동그라미가 꽃이 되고
어느 때는 무심코 옆으로 그린 직선이
하늘과 땅이 만나는 곳이 된다

나는 스케치를 하면서
앙상한 나뭇가지들을 잠깐 바라본다
종이 위에 그린 직선들은 아침햇살이 되고
장미 넝쿨의 가시가 된다

꽃들이 환하게 핀다

장미가시들은 호수 깊이 잠든 추억처럼
고기 지느러미를 꿰뚫는 핀으로 바뀐다

백합꽃이 숲에 숨어서
수줍게 웃고 있다

나는 비발디의 사계를 듣는다

밖에는 비가 내리고 있다
세찬 바람이 나를 감싸고 번개가 치고
커다란 천둥소리가 들린다

바로 그 순간 전등이 꺼진다
모든 것이 어둠 속으로 사라진다
나는 촛불을 켜고 다시 시작한다

빈 종이에다 연필을 갖다 댄다

Mummy Entreats

In a showcase of dim light
her gloomy smile captivates me.
A pale ashen-brown prehistoric mummy
lies face up on a table.
Her long black hair winds around her neck
covered in a dark green linen muffler.
Discolored teeth distorted in her open mouth.
But her face has not lost its contours, its beauty once perceived.

Beside her body lies a gold chain, jade earrings and green precious stones—
objects that indicate she was a high-ranking imperial princess.
Still, from the blood stains on her ragged jacket,
I suspect her last moments were tragic
and her final cries reach out to me in the silence.

When my eyes meet her eyes she pathetically vindicates herself.
She who was falsely accused of rebellion and then died.
Regardless of the explanation I read on the display case label
she might have been wrongly accused by rogues or schemers.

In the futilities of her life sometimes there were good seasons:
When maidservants ornamented her face and body
with jewels and perfumes…
But all vanished in a moment.
Only these articles remain as eyewitness.

Imagining the last day of the princess
I am pushed from the showcase by a crowd of visitors.
Though I leave the museum, her piercing cries follow me.

애원하는 미라

어두운 불빛 아래 진열장 속
그녀의 침울한 미소를 넋을 잃고 바라본다
선사시대의 잿빛 갈색의 창백한 미라가
천장을 향해 테이블에 누워있다
검은 아마 섬유 목도리를 한 목에는
그녀의 긴 머리칼이 감겨 있다
벌어진 입 속에 뒤틀리고 탈색된 이빨들이 보인다
그러나 얼굴 윤곽은 남아있어
그녀가 한때 미인이었음을 알 수 있다

그녀 곁에는 금으로 만든 목걸이
비취로 만든 귀걸이와 녹색 빛나는 보석들
그녀가 고귀한 신분의 황녀였음을
알게 해 주는 물건들이 놓여있다
너덜너덜해진 그녀의 상의에 아직도
남아있는 혈흔을 보고 그녀의
최후의 순간들이 비극적이었을 거라 생각하니
그녀의 마지막 외침이 조용히 들려온다

내 눈이 그녀의 눈과 마주칠 때 그녀는 진열장
표지판에 적혀 있는 설명과는 무관하게 반역의
누명을 쓰고 목숨을 잃었다고 애원하듯 주장한다
그녀는 악당들이나 모사꾼들로부터
누명을 썼을 지도 모른다

허무하게 끝난 그녀의 삶에서 그녀의 몸종들이
그녀의 얼굴과 몸을 보석과 향수로 장식해주던
좋은 시절이 있었을 것이다
그러나 모든 것이 일순간에 사라지고
그때의 장식품들만 증거로 남아있다

그녀의 마지막 날을 상상해 보면서
나는 수많은 사람들에 떠밀려 진열장을 떠난다
박물관을 떠나도 그녀의 날카로운 외침이
나를 따라온다

Ruby

I'm reading a book on American history.
My wife's asleep
under the lamp's red-shaded glow.

On Hollywood's red carpet
Marilyn Monroe's scarlet lipstick
outlines her sunny smile. Her cheeks are rouged too.

She arranges a red ribbon in the lapel of her jacket;
wears high-heeled shoes, the color of fire.
A crimson-capped young girl presents a bouquet of burgundy roses.

Outside the Stars and Stripes wave in the wind.

Suddenly a shot is heard from a car in Dallas.
Blood, ruby-red, pours from President John F. Kennedy.

His wife, Jacqueline, cries out loudly.
Later, a single red rose is placed on the grave.

루비

나는 미국 역사책을 읽고 있다
아내는 붉은빛 전등 갓 아래
잠들어 있다

할리우드 레드카펫 위에
주홍 색 립스틱으로
마릴린 먼로의 밝은 미소가 그려져 있다
그녀 뺨에도 루주가 칠해져 있다

그녀는 상의 옷깃에 붉은 리본을 달고
불꽃 색깔의 하이힐을 신고 있다
진홍 모자를 쓴 소녀가 진홍색
장미꽃다발을 건네 준다

밖에는 미국 국기가 펄럭이고 있다

갑자기 댈러스의 승용차에서
총성이 들려온다
존 에프 케네디 대통령이 붉은 피를 쏟고

영부인 재클린이 대성통곡을 한다
얼마 후 붉은 장미 한 송이가
무덤에 놓인다

The Border

Monterey weather is calm and free.
Seaside aquarium crowded with visitors.
Schools of fish are swimming
inside the border.

A crowd of anchovy are dancing quickly like one
according to the fish trainer's intention.
No one is falling into disorder.

A sea otter's infant is playing ball,
sucking milk from his mother's breast.
The infant doesn't even know the visitors,
is not interested.

But mother sea otter looks anxious,
keeps a sharp lookout.
Her heart is outside in the immense blue ocean.

Inside, a lonely island!
Sealed despair.
Nostalgia's flag!

Tender affections keep hearts beating.
She misses her childhood in the vast ocean, her birthplace.
Never thinks of that windstorm night
when she was caught by fishermen.

In the outside border
children are chattering continually.
The youngest and the oldest are observing
inside the aquarium closely.
Infants are playing with rattles,
sucking milk from their mothers' breasts.

경계선

몬테레이 날씨는 온화하고 자유롭다
바닷가 수족관은 방문객들로 붐빈다
경계선 안쪽에는 고기떼가 헤엄친다

큰 무리의 멸치들이 조련사의 뜻에 따라
단 한 마리도 이탈하지 않고
마치 한 몸처럼 재빠르게 춤을 춘다

새끼 수달이 공을 갖고 놀면서
어미젖을 빨고 있다.
새끼는 방문객들을 알지도 못하고 관심도 없다

그러나 어미 수달은 불안한 눈으로
날카롭게 경계를 한다
어미의 마음은 광대한 푸른 바다에 가 있다

경계선 안쪽은
외로운 섬 감금된 절망
향수의 깃발!

부드러운 사랑이 가슴을 뛰게 한다
어미 수달은 광대한 고향 바다에서 보낸
유년시절을 그리워한다
어부들에게 붙잡힌 폭풍우 몰아치던 밤을
절대 회상하지 않는다

경계선 밖에서는 아이들이
끊임없이 재잘대고 있다
가장 어린 애와 가장 나이 많은 애가
수족관 속을 유심히 들여다보고 있다
갓난애들은 딸랑이를 흔들며
엄마 젖을 빨고 있다

Everybody takes great pleasure
from the inside border.
By the fish and the sea otters' sacrifice
they are enjoying.
By another's sacrifice we are taking happiness.

Inside and outside.
Ourselves and others.
The border,
Who made it?

모두가 경계선 안을 바라보며
매우 즐거워한다
물고기와 수달로 그들은 즐거워하고
다른 사람들의 희생으로
우리는 행복을 누리고 있다

안과 밖
우리와 다른 사람들
그 경계를 누가 만들었나

I Didn't Know That Before

I didn't know that before.
I never expected it before.
I didn't realize that you were going to leave
without saying a word.

So vain, how did you heartlessly leave without a sound?
Was there anything so urgent
that you could not say goodbye?

My beloved gone.

I call your name
to an empty field.
I loudly call your name out into the air.

Our firmly sworn promise
like a handful of dust
floats away in the breeze.

You appeared for a little while.
Now faded away like mist.

You'll never know I've loved you endlessly.

As you go through the years
you may repent.
Call me anytime.

Though you may look shabby,
I'll be there to wrap your broken heart.

You left, but cross-way whispers of love between us
come back
like an echo that fills a void.

미처 몰랐습니다

미처 몰랐습니다
결코 예상하지 못했습니다
그대가 한마디 말도 없이
떠날 줄 몰랐습니다

허무하게 어찌 그리 소리도 없이
매정하게 떠나셨습니까?
무슨 급한 일이 있었기에
작별인사도 없이 떠나셨습니까?

나의 사랑은 떠나갔습니다

텅 빈 들을 향해
그대 이름을 불러봅니다
허공에 대고 그대
이름을 소리쳐 불러봅니다

우리들이 굳게 맺은 언약은
한줌의 먼지처럼
미풍 속에 사라졌습니다

그대는 잠시 나타났다
안개처럼 사라졌습니다

그대는 내가 그대를
끝없이 사랑했다는 것을
결코 알 수 없을 것입니다

세월이 가면
그대는 후회하실 겁니다
아무 때라도 불러주세요

비록 그대가 초라해 보일지라도
나는 그대의 상처받은 가슴을
감싸 안아 줄 것입니다

그대는 떠나갔지만
우리가 나눈 사랑의 속삭임은
허공을 채우는 메아리처럼 되돌아옵니다

Though She Left Me

Once I tried hard to escape from remembering,
but the harder I struggled, the more I was reminded.
It was no use making the effort.

We vowed not to say farewell.
I knew it was no use crying.

Though she left me,
her bright eyes, glowing cheeks and opulent lips
live in my heart.
Her sweet voice and dimpled smile
are with me too.

Memories of McDonalds, Starbucks,
and midnight movies are still with me.
The beaches of Waikiki we visited during summer vacation.
Central Park in autumn, trees ablaze with color.
Fallen leaves on the roadsides.
Blue sky over the snowy mountain.

The leaves are all off the trees and have traveled the globe.
Although our love may be buried
together with leaves,
her bright eyes, glowing cheeks and
opulent lips are still in my heart,
still alive in me.
Along with my fervent yearning.

그녀는 떠나갔지만

한때는 추억에서 벗어나고 싶었습니다
그러나 벗어나려고 애쓸수록
더 벗어날 수 없었습니다
아무리 노력을 해도 소용이 없었습니다

우리는 이별을 말하지 않기로 약속했습니다
울어도 소용없다는 걸 알았습니다

그녀는 떠나갔지만
그 빛나는 눈동자 복숭앗빛 두 뺨
화려한 입술은 내 가슴에 남아있습니다
고운 목소리 보조개 미소도 내게 남아있습니다

맥도날드 스타벅스 그리고 야간 상영 영화들에
대한 추억도 내게 남아있습니다
여름휴가 때 함께 갔던 와이키키 해변
가을의 센트럴 파크 단풍나무 길가 낙엽
그리고 눈 덮인 산 위의 푸른 하늘

나뭇잎은 모두 떨어져 어디론가 사라졌습니다
우리의 사랑이 나뭇잎에 파묻힌다 해도
그 빛나는 눈동자 복숭앗빛 두 뺨
화려한 입술은 내 가슴에 남아있습니다
그대를 애타게 그리는 내 가슴에 남아있습니다

At Abbotts Lagoon Beach

Here the reeds in the field are tossed about by winds.
Like an army of men in tasseled hats marching forward.

Swayed toward one side.
They do not behave themselves
against the winds.
They prefer to stand upright
to talk with heaven.
But winds pull them continuously
to go in their direction.

Sometimes when it is blowing a gale they weep loudly.
And when it rains they are filled with water.

The weather on this beach is frequently changing.
But always this salty breeze and humid air remains.
After suffering day and night, from winds in all directions
the heads of these reeds cannot help but hang down.

Calmly night falls here.
The whitish salt fields' panorama
spread out
beside the beach
flooded all over
with brilliant moonlight.

애보츠 라군 해변에서

이곳 들판에는 모자에 술을 단 군인들이
앞으로 나아가듯 갈대들이 바람에 휩쓸린다

갈대들이 한쪽으로 휩쓸린다
갈대들은 바람 앞에서 얌전하게 행동하지 않는다
갈대들은 하늘과 대화하려고
똑바로 서있는 걸 더 좋아한다
그러나 바람은 갈대들을 계속해서
바람의 방향으로만 잡아당긴다

때때로 강풍이 불 때면
갈대들은 큰 소리로 운다
그리고 비가 올 때면 갈대들은
비에 흠뻑 젖는다

이 해변의 날씨는 수시로 바뀌지만
소금기 머금은 미풍과 습한 공기는
언제나 해변에 남아있다
사방에서 불어오는 바람에 밤낮으로 시달리고 난
갈대들은 결국 고개를 숙일 수밖에 없다

이곳에 조용하게 밤이 찾아오고
희끄무레한 소금 밭 전경이
밝은 달빛 넘치는 해변에 펼쳐진다

Fireflies in the Backyard

In the soft summer New Jersey night
fireflies in my backyard
flitting here and there
illuminating the blackness.

Each summer the fireflies return
reminding me of my childhood in Korea
in the rural community
where we were too poor to buy light.

Sometimes too poor to own a candle,
we collected fireflies in a basket
and read books by their sparks.

Fireflies delightedly giving off their radiance
brightening the dark garden.

뒷마당의 반딧불이

뉴저지의 포근한 여름 밤
뒷마당에서 반딧불이들이
어둠을 밝히며
이리저리 날아다닌다

여름이면 반딧불이들이 찾아와
가난 때문에 등불도 못 켜고 살았던
코리아의 시골 고향집을 생각나게 한다

때로는 양초 살 돈도 없어
반딧불이들을 바구니에 담아
그 반짝이는 빛에 책을 읽었다

반딧불이들은 그들의 빛을
기꺼이 내주어 어두운 정원을
밝혀주고 있다

A Heavy Silence

Between Powell Station and Aquatic Park
an old woman is dragged off a crowded Muni bus
—the Number 30—
by tall and sturdy policemen—one on each side.

With no money for a ticket
she is silent;
a lamb before slaughter,
a sheep before it is sheared.

With no money for proper clothing
she is dressed in rags.
Her thinning white hair
like the root of an onion.

She joins her hands together
in prayer and supplication.
Begs pardon with her tears.

She retreats
with a wagon filled with vegetables—parsnips and turnips.
A walking stick in her hand
insufficient to aid her.

The passengers on the bus
watch transfixed.
An old woman
bent with worry and fear,
and making little progress.

Thinking hard, no one says a word.
And the bus is filled with a heavy silence.

무거운 침묵

파월 스테이션과 아쿠아틱 파크 사이
할머니 한 분이
키 크고 건장한 경찰관 두 사람에게 팔이 잡혀
30번 시영버스에서 끌려 나온다

무일푼인 그녀는 버스표 살 돈이 없다
그녀는 마치 백정이나 양털 깎는
사람 앞에 선 양처럼 말이 없다

누더기를 걸친 그녀의 숱이 적은
머리는 양파뿌리처럼 하얗다

기도를 하듯 애원을 하듯
두 손을 모은다
눈물로 용서를 빈다

그녀는 무와 미나리를 가득
실은 수레를 끌기 시작한다
한 손에 지팡이를 쥐었지만 걷는데
별 도움이 안 된다

승객들은 걱정과 두려움으로 그녀를 꼼짝 않고
바라보지만 아무도 나서질 않는다

속으로 생각은 많이 하지만
입 밖으로 말을 꺼내는 사람은 없다
버스에는 무거운 침묵만이 흐른다

A Lucky Day

All through the morning, every day, an obscure saxophone player in New York City wanders from place to place, setting up stage in Times Square, the Port Authority Bus Terminal, Grand Central Station or the Empire State Building.

He places his worn-out hat (his only other possession) upturned,
in front of his feet.
With closed eyes he performs his favorite songs:
Oh Happy Day and *Gypsy's Nostalgia.*

Immersed in the playing he forgets his hunger, sorrow and loneliness.
When he plays the saxophone, it doesn't matter who listens.
But a lucky day is to hear loud applause from the audience.

운이 좋은 날

날이면 날마다 아침이 오면
이름 없는 색소폰 연주자는
타임스 스퀘어, 항만관리 버스터미널,
그랜드 센트럴 스테이션, 엠파이어스테이트 빌딩을
옮겨 다니며 무대를 차려 놓고 색소폰을 연주한다

그는 발 아래 그에게 하나뿐인
낡은 모자를 뒤집어 놓고
눈을 감고 그가 가장 좋아하는 "오, 해피데이" 와
"집시 노스탤지어"를 연주한다

연주에 심취한 그는 배고픔도
슬픔도 외로움도 잊는다
색소폰을 연주할 때는
듣는 사람이 누구든 상관없다
그러나 운이 좋은 날에는
청중으로부터 큰 박수를 받는다

Doorman

It is said that the first job the apartment doorman got
is the job he tried so hard to achieve for several years.

It is said he has never sat on a chair while working his shift
from six o'clock in the morning until ten o'clock at night,
arriving at the office before anyone else and leaving last.

It is said that he even eats lunch while standing up,
chewing his hamburger with one eye on the door,
eating hastily without any drink.

It is said by some people that when he uses the toilet
he must relieve himself in a few seconds,
he returns to his post so soon.

It is said he always smiles and greets the residents with a humble bow,
bowing down even to their dogs.

It is said he has never even applied for a leave
or taken a vacation.

It is said he has changed, become an old man too early, stooped with age;
that his face was altered,
that once he had a big smile.

But now he is like a mannequin
with only a resolute grin.

도어 맨

아파트 도어 맨은 첫 직장을 잡을 때까지
수년 동안 정말 힘들게 노력했다고 한다

아침 6시 출근, 밤 10시 퇴근 때까지
가장 먼저 출근해 가장 늦게 퇴근하면서
근무시간에는 의자에 한번 앉지도 않고
일한다고 한다

점심 먹을 때도 한눈으로는 문을 응시하느라
앉지도 못하고 서서 허겁지겁 햄버거를 먹으며
음료수도 마시지 못한다고 한다

몇몇 사람들이 말하길 그가 화장실에 갈 때는
단 몇 초 만에 용변을 마치고 금방 제자리로
돌아온다고 한다

그는 항상 웃고 입주자들에게 정중히 인사하고
입주자들이 키우는 개한테도 인사를 한다고 한다

그는 한 번도 휴가신청을 하지 않고
휴가도 가지 않는다고 한다

그러나 이제 그는 변했고 너무 일찍 늙어버려
나이 들수록 등이 굽고
함박웃음 짓던 얼굴은 변해

마네킹처럼 판에 박힌
웃음만 짓는 사람이 되었다

No Friend But a Stick

Among the people strolling in the park
a pedestrian walks with a stick.
Doing his best, moving little by little.

With each step he takes, the upper part of his body collapses.
His only friend, the stick, used like a cane,
gives him the courage to stand up again.
And he struggles to his feet each time.

He continues this unnatural walking
diligently with absolute quiet.
As a pure white butterfly
follows behind.

While treading slowly, step-by-step,
other people easily move ahead of him.
He stops and stares vacantly at the empty sky,
recalling nostalgic moments of bygone days
when he walked like others.

유일한 친구 지팡이

공원을 산책하는 사람 중
한 보행자가 지팡이를 짚고
최선을 다해 조금씩 걷는다

한 걸음씩 뗄 때마다 앞으로 구부러진다
그가 지팡이로 삼는 그의 유일한 벗인
지팡이가 다시 일어날 용기를 준다

그가 이 부자연스러운 걷기를
무거운 침묵 속에 계속하는 동안
하얀 나비 한 마리가 그의 뒤를 따른다

그가 천천히 한 걸음 한 걸음씩 걸을 때
다른 사람들은 쉽게 그를 앞서간다
그는 멈춰 서서 멍하니 빈 하늘을 바라보고
남들처럼 걸었던 옛날에 대한 추억에 젖는다

What is Seen

On my way home from work at the office
I stand reading a book in the aisle of the crowded subway.
Many more passengers are standing than sitting.

In a seat reserved for the disabled
a young couple watches a smartphone screen together
dressed alike in baseball caps and jean jackets

connected by a single set of headphones…
Arm in arm they are laughing together.
Almost one being.

Beside them, a snowy-haired grandmother stands
clutching the corner of the seat.
Limp and pale, she carries her burden—
a sack over her left shoulder.

At the next station a graceful and healthy woman gets on.
Seeing the young couple in the handicapped seat
she flashes her senior identification.

She sends them on their way.
Settling in with dignity.

The subway train continues to its final destination.
All of us will disembark soon.

보이는 것

사무실에서 일을 마치고 돌아오는 길에
지하철 복도 승객들 틈에 서서 책을 읽는다
앉아있는 사람보다 서 있는 사람이 더 많다

장애인석에 젊은 남녀가 앉아
함께 스마트폰을 보고 있다

둘 다 야구모자와 진 재킷을 입은 남녀는
헤드폰을 한쪽씩 나눠 끼고 있다

그들 옆에는 다리를 저는
창백한 얼굴에 눈처럼 하얀 머리의
할머니 한 분이 좌석 한 모퉁이를 붙잡고 서 있다
할머니는 왼쪽 어깨에 자루 짐까지 메고 있다

다음 역에서 우아하고 건장한 여인이 승차하더니
경로 우대증을 꺼내 장애인석에 앉아있는
젊은 남녀에게 보인 다음

그들을 다른 데로 보내고
점잖게 자리를 차지한다

지하철은 종착역을 향해가고
우리 모두는 곧 하차하게 될 것이다

Meteor Shower at Inwood Hill Park

In upper Manhattan one summer evening
I lie on the ground and look up at the sky;
Beyond the city lights, a myriad of stars and nebulae visible in the darkness.

Several meteors appear and disappear, like flickering lights.
While stationary stars like Polaris and the Big Dipper
hang on in the glittering sky.

Meteors appear and disappear
in the twinkling of an eye.
I imagine that our life is also a flash in an eternity.

인우드 힐 공원의 유성우

어느 여름날 저녁 북부 맨해튼에서
땅바닥에 누워 하늘을 쳐다보다가
도시의 불빛 너머 어둠 속에서
수많은 별과 성운을 발견한다

북극성이나 북두칠성처럼 움직이지 않는 별들은
빛나는 하늘에서 제자리를 지키고 있는데
몇 개의 유성들은 깜박이는 등불처럼
나타났다가 사라진다

눈 깜짝할 사이에 나타났다 사라지는 유성들
영원의 시간에 비하면 우리의 삶도
이들과 다를 게 무엇인가

The Snail

After an evening of slight rain
a snail tries to move
in haste.

But slowly creeps
on the leaf
of a morning glory.

With tentacles for eyes
its pace
is slow,
intermittent
even…

This snail seems to think
before reaching its conclusion—
to move
from the old to the new.

North to south
forest floor to a peak of ocean
from fine to windy days.

Leaving a glimmer of itself,
marking a trail for others to follow.

A snail carries its universe
within a spiral-shaped shell—
with all its thoughts and necessities.

Spending its effort all alone
preoccupied with moving to the next place only.
Solving its problems slowly.

달팽이

가랑비가 조금 내린 뒤
달팽이가 움직이려고 서둘러서
나팔꽃 위를 느리게 기어간다

그러나 눈 대신 사용하는 더듬이를
간헐적으로 사용하니
움직임이 느리다

달팽이는 전의 곳에서
새로운 곳으로 가는 것을 생각하고

남에서 북으로
숲 바닥에서 바다로, 청명한 날로부터
바람 부는 날로 간다고
생각하는 것 같다

달팽이는 희미하게 보이는
고유한 표식을 남겨
다른 달팽이들이
뒤를 따라올 수 있게 한다

달팽이는 나선형 모양의 집 속에
모든 생각과 필요한 것들을 포함한
자신의 우주를 담아 운반한다

달팽이는 다음에 이동할 장소를 미리 생각하고
자신의 문제들을 자신만의 힘으로
천천히 해결해 나간다

The Patience of Heron

A white heron waits tranquilly for fish in a stream.
Not fussy about what size or type of fish
he waits.

Standing steady for an hour,
calmly, in an upright position.
So serene that even his breath seems to cease.

Slowly he bends his long neck.
The tasseled hairs on his head erect
as if imploring even the winds not to move.

He continues waiting until the fish come
then he shifts with lightning speed to catch it.

Biting the fish with his bill.
His mouth closed.
He waits while the fish writhes in agony.

He just keeps on waiting until the fish is completely exhausted.
Sometimes the fish is bigger than his head.
But he gradually swallows it wholly without chewing.

백로의 인내심

백로 한 마리가 개울물에서
조용히 고기를 기다린다
고기의 크기나 종류를 가리지 않고 기다린다

똑바로 서서 미동도 하지 않고
한 시간 동안 한결같이
숨도 안 쉬는 듯 조용히 기다린다

바람에게도 움직이지 말라고 애원하는 듯
제 머리에 난 깃털을 똑바로 세우고
긴 목을 구부린다

백로는 고기가 나오기를 계속 기다리다가
번개 같은 속도로 움직여 고기를 잡는다

고기를 부리로 물고
고기가 고통에 몸부림치는 동안
입을 다물고 기다린다

백로는 고기가 몸부림치다
완전히 지칠 때까지 기다린다
백로의 머리보다 더 큰 고기라도
백로는 씹지 않고 통째로 천천히 삼킨다

Squirrel

The squirrel is always so inquisitive about everything—
looking around restlessly while coming and going.

With his paws behind his ears he tries to hear the sounds
of the wind and the birdsong, even my breath.

Continually jumping up and down—
changing his steps and the movement of his tail.
His body is lighter than air and softer than shadows.

Stealthy and furtive he walks quietly on the wind.
He moves shrewdly to transcend time and space.

Squirrel leisurely tilts his head and effortlessly walks the high-wire above.
Like a ping-pong ball he moves from branch to branch, tree to tree.

When he scurries down the aspen to look at me
he is burning with the same curiosity about me
as I feel for him.

For a little while the wind, birdsong, even breath
all seem to cease.
Even the second hand on the clock is still.

다람쥐

다람쥐는 언제나 모든 것에 호기심을 갖고
이리저리 움직이며 쉬지 않고 주변을 두리번거린다

앞발을 귀에 대고 바람소리 새소리 나의
숨소리까지도 귀 기울여 듣는다

펄쩍펄쩍 뛰기를 계속하며
발걸음과 꼬리를 이리저리 움직인다
몸은 공기보다 가볍고
꼬리는 그림자보다 더 부드럽다

다람쥐는 몰래 살그머니
바람을 타고 걷는 것 같다
마치 시간과 공간을 초월하는 것처럼
약삭빠르게 움직인다

다람쥐는 한가롭게 머리를
한쪽으로 기울이기도 하고
높은 줄 위를 부드럽게 걷기도 하며
탁구공처럼 나뭇가지 사이를 이동한다

나무에서 내려와 불타는 듯한 호기심으로
나를 바라볼 때면
나는 다람쥐에게 연민을 느낀다

잠시 바람과 새소리 나의 숨소리
손목시계 초침까지도
모두 잠깐 멈추는 듯하다

Deer

Without a sound she comes to my backyard
and like a shadow she disappears.
She is always silent.

She has no antlers, but two fawns.
Her quiet vigilance keeps them cozy,
as if they are still in the womb.

The mother's affection draws
the depth of the deep ocean
and her dark eyes hug them warmly.

She looks blankly at her shadow through the window
seeming to recollect her mate who has fled
leaving her with two little ones.

She has many things to mutter against him
but only chews over the good.
Ruminating the cud again and again.

사슴

소리도 없이 나의 집 뒷마당으로 왔다가
그림자처럼 사라지는 사슴은
언제나 조용하다

뿔은 없고 새끼가 두 마리인데
어미가 소리 없이 경계를 서주니
새끼들은 어미 뱃속만큼 편하다

어미의 새끼 사랑은
깊은 바다만큼 깊어 새끼들을
눈으로 따뜻하게 포옹한다

유리 창문을 통해 자신의 그림자를
멍하니 바라보는 사슴은
새끼 두 마리를 남기고 떠나간
제 짝을 생각하는 듯

떠나간 짝에 대해 불평할 게 많지만
좋았던 일들만 회상하며
되새김질을 반복한다

Dolphin

You yearn to return home—
The way the night watchman waits for the morning.
But your dream is pathetic.

You are hungry and hanker for affection.
You stave off this famine with the anchovies
fed to you after you perform for the spectators.

In the aquarium you do flips, play ball and jump through hoops—
exercises you have practiced daily.
You really don't like entertaining,
but you do it to appease your desire.

You are my lovely friend.
A lover longing for the wide freedom of the ocean.
When will you return home?

돌고래

야간 경비원이 아침을 기다리듯
고향으로 돌아가고 싶어하는
너의 꿈이 가련하다

배고픔과 사랑에 대한 갈망을 안고
관중들을 위한 공연이 끝난 뒤
네게 주어지는 멸치로 기아를 쫓는 너

수족관에서 뒤집기 공 다루기
둥근 테 통과하기 등 네가 매일 하는 연기는
관중을 즐겁게 해주기 위해서라기보다
너의 배고픔을 해결하기 위한 것

너는 사랑스러운 나의 친구
대양을 마음껏 헤엄치는 꿈을 가진 나의 애인
언제쯤 고향에 돌아 가려나

Invisible Leash

At the training center a dog is tied to a stake—
a taut leash restrains him.

All day long he keeps trying to go further away
as if there were some chance of escape.

Sometimes he seems to forget his shackles.
And suddenly he rushes forward quickly.

But each time the leash tightens even more
and his body is jerked into the air.

Although he struggles with every fiber of his being, the distance
he can move is not increased or decreased, and he seems diminished.

Today, the dog's trainer unties his leash.
At first the dog refuses to run forward—but leaps furiously in place.

Then, even after he goes out a sizable distance, he returns.
There is no leash now, but the distance between dog and stake is still taut.

보이지 않는 끈

개 훈련장에 개 한 마리가 말뚝에
팽팽한 끈으로 매어 있다

도망을 칠 수라도 있는 것처럼
멀리 벗어나려 온종일 애를 쓴다

종종 목에 채워진 족쇄를 잊어버린 듯
갑자기 재빨리 앞으로 돌진한다

그러나 그때마다 족쇄는 더 조여지고
개의 몸은 공중에서 홱 잡아당겨진다

개가 그 존재의 마지막 힘까지 다해 보아도
움직일 수 있는 거리는 늘지도 않고
줄지도 않아 위축되기만 할 뿐

오늘은 개 훈련사가 개 끈을 풀어주니
처음에는 앞으로 달려 나가지 않다가
나중에는 제자리에서 무섭게 뛴다

그러더니 상당한 거리를 나간 후에도
원래 있던 자리로 돌아온다
개 끈이 없어도 개와 말뚝 사이의 거리는
팽팽하게 당겨져 있다

Wandering Earthworms

On a summer morning, earthworms appear here and there
on the pathways where many people are coming and going.
The pedestrians do not mind the earthworms beneath their feet
keeping obsessively busy from sunup to late at night they haven't time to notice.

Earthworms might come out from their burrows to migrate or mate
not perceiving the serious danger they pose to pedestrians.
They might be searching for friends or families
wandering alone and roaming from place to place.

I imagine that someone could show them the best path to take…
Much as the creator looking at our lives might feel,
observing billions of humans who move around the world
without knowing death may be imminent in any given moment.

헤매는 지렁이들

여름아침 많은 사람들이 오고 가는 길
여기저기에 지렁이들이 나타난다
사람들은 아침부터 밤 늦게까지 바빠
그들 발 밑에 있는 지렁이들을 살펴볼
시간적 여유도 없고 신경도 쓰지 못한다

그들은 보행자들로부터 받는 심각한 위험을
감지하지 못한 채 다른 곳으로 이동하거나
짝짓기를 위해 땅에서 밖으로 나왔을 것이다
친구나 가족을 찾기 위해 외롭게 방황하며
이리저리 돌아다닐 것이다

어느 순간에 죽을지도 모르고
세상곳곳을 돌아다니는 수십억 인간들의
삶을 보시고 창조주께서 느끼실 것처럼
누군가 지렁이들에게 최선의 길을 보여준다면
어떨까 하는 상상을 해본다

Imprisoned Words

Impatient and perplexed,
persistently scratching the floor with her claws.

Her large eyes
seem to speak
something urgent and painful.

But I have no ears to hear it.

All her requests to me, everything she wants,
seems to be in her eyes.
The words held back like tears that don't spill out.

Words that can find no way to come.

Even though she is making an appeal
still there is no sound; still the words
do not budge.

What can I do?
Only pass my hand over her head repeatedly.
Make a trip to a veterinarian.

Who can open the prison
that has confined these words
for millions of years?

막혀 있는 말

애완견이 당혹감과 초조함으로
바닥을 계속 발톱으로 할퀴고 있다

커다란 눈은 무언가
절박한 고통을 말하고 있는데

나는 그걸 들을 수가 없다

나에게 하는 부탁과 나에게 원하는 게
모두 애완견의 눈 속에 있지만
흘러내리지 않는 눈물처럼 그의 말문은 막혀 있다

말이 나올 길이 없다

무언가 호소를 하고 있지만
소리는 없다
말로 표현되는 건 전혀 없다

내가 무얼 할 수 있나
그의 머리를 반복해서 쓰다듬어 줄 수 있을 뿐
이제는 수의사에게 데리고 가야겠다

수백만 년 동안 막힌 애완견의 말문을
누가 터줄 수 있을 것인가

You Are Mine

Every Wednesday Mrs. Brown frequents the grooming salon at PetSmart.
Though she makes an appointment, the salon is always busy.

She takes her poodle, Eddy, for a haircut.
Sometimes a bath, blow dry and brush.
Nails manicured, polished, trimmed, all included in the price of the service.
For a healthy smile, she cleans Eddy's teeth at home every day.
Bathes Eddy with her shampoo, dries his body;
massages his coat with a mixture of jojoba oil,
chamomile and aloe for a light finish.
She puts a pink ribbon in Eddy's hair, red shoes on his paws.

When she goes out she always puts shoes on the poodle—
in spite of Eddy's groans.
She puts a striped jacket on Eddy's back
even in sultry weather.
On sunny days she puts sunglasses on Eddy.
All his accessories are changed according to her desires, not Eddy's.

Mrs. Brown had a veterinarian cut Eddy's tail for a beauty show.
She almost had the vet cut off part of his ears!

She never thinks about Eddy's feelings at all.
She believes that Eddy belongs to her.
And doesn't think about the animate creature.

When a rainy day comes
Eddy turns round and round repeatedly.
Seeking a trace of his tail.

너는 나의 것

매주 수요일에 브라운 여사는
페트마트에 있는 털 손질 가게에 간다
예약을 하지만 가게는 항상 붐빈다

그녀는 그녀의 푸들 에디의 털을 깎으려고 간다
때로는 목욕을 시켜 말리고 솔질을 하려고 간다
손톱을 다듬고 매니큐어를 칠하고 윤을 내는
비용이 모두 봉사료에 포함돼 있다
개가 웃을 때 건강하게 보이려고 그녀는
에디의 이빨을 매일 집에서 닦아준다
자신의 샴푸로 에디를 목욕시킨 다음
몸을 말려주고 호호바오일 혼합물로 털을
마사지해 주고 카모마일과 알로에로 가볍게 마감한다
머리에는 분홍색 리본을 달아주고
발에는 빨간 신발을 신겼다

그녀가 외출할 때면 개가 신음소리를 내도
그녀는 어김없이 개에게 신발을 신긴다
푹푹 찌는 무더운 날씨에도 그녀는 에디의
등에다 줄무늬가 있는 옷을 입힌다
화창한 날씨에는 에디에게 색안경을 쓰게 한다
모든 액세서리는 개의 욕망이 아니라
그녀의 욕망에 따라 바뀐다

브라운 여사는 예쁜 개를 뽑는 대회에
에디를 내보내기 위해 수의사를 시켜
에디의 꼬리를 자르게 했다
하마터면 그녀는 수의사를 시켜
개의 귀 일부를 자를 뻔했다

그녀는 에디의 감정을 고려하는 법이 없다
그녀는 에디가 그녀의 소유물이라고 믿기에
에디의 처지를 생각하지 않는다

비 오는 날이면 에디는 자신의 꼬리
흔적을 찾으려고 반복해서 돌고 또 돈다

Hamlet Park Afternoon

Five-o-clock in the afternoon:
A village whose people love dogs.

Every afternoon big dogs out taking a walk with their people.
Sometimes the dogs and their masters just ahead of me...

Dogs let loose in a patch of grass.
Dogs move their bowels once free.

A Bulldog barks at a Greyhound for some reason.
A small mongrel wags its tail, sniffing another dog's anus.

A maiden embracing a poodle
enters the park.
Teenagers shouting to a Shepherd,
tossing a Frisbee to train him.

A middle-aged man in a blue beret
walks five dogs
past the children's playground.
The dragon tattoo on his forearm
bulging as he tries to restrain them.

A gray-haired couple
arrives at the entrance.
Disappointment and fear on their faces—
so many dogs!

A young woman pushes a baby carriage,
walking gingerly with her Boxer.

The sun sets behind the western mountains.
And the round full moon rises in the east.

작은 마을 공원의 오후

오후 5시
개를 사랑하는 사람들이 사는 마을

매일 오후면 커다란 개들이
주인들과 산책을 하러 나온다
때로는 개들과 개 주인들이 바로 내 앞에서 걷는다

잔디밭에 풀어놓은 개들
개들은 일단 풀어놓으면 변을 본다

무슨 이유인지 불도그가
그레이하운드를 보고 짖는다
작은 잡종개가 꼬리를 흔들며
다른 개 항문에 코를 대고 쿵쿵거린다

푸들을 안은 처녀가 공원으로 들어온다
십대들이 셰퍼드를 훈련시키려고
원반을 던지며 개에게 소리를 친다

푸른 베레모를 쓴 중년남자가
개 다섯 마리를 끌고 어린이 운동장을
지나간다 개들을 제지하려고 할 때
그의 팔뚝에 새겨진 용의 문신이 부풀어 오른다

백발 노부부가 공원입구에 도착한다
그들의 얼굴에 나타나는 실망감과 두려움
이렇게나 개가 많다니!

유모차를 미는 젊은 여인이
복서 한 마리를 데리고 조심스레 걸어간다

태양은 서산으로 지고
둥근 달이 동쪽에서 떠오른다

Puberty

The weather is fine today
but yesterday was windy with rain.
The day before yesterday was also stormy.

Due to recent unexpected changes
it is not possible to forecast what the weather will be.

Today Emily didn't go to school;
and she didn't eat anything.
The day before yesterday she didn't go either,
but that was because of the rain.

Lately she received high scores in mathematics
but still was not happy. Sometimes she
convulses with laughter in her room or
whimpers without reason.

Sensitive to every little whisper
she responds with a scream.

Stifling his emotions, Emily's father firmly kicks
a rugby ball around the playground.
Uncertain where it will land.

사춘기

오늘은 날씨가 좋다
그러나 어제는 비가 오고 바람이 불었다
그저께도 역시 폭풍우가 몰아쳤다

최근 예상치 못한 기후변화로
날씨를 예측하기 불가능해졌다

오늘은 에밀리가 학교에 가지 않고
밥도 먹지 않았다
그저께도 학교에 가지 않았는데
그건 비가 왔기 때문이다

최근에 그녀는 수학에서 높은 점수를
받았지만 기뻐하지 않았다
근래에 와서 그녀는 그녀 방에서
포복절도를 하며 웃는가 하면
아무 이유도 없이 훌쩍거린다

작은 속삭임에도 민감하게
반응해 소리를 지른다

에밀리 아빠는 감정을 억누르고 운동장에 나가
어디로 날아갈지도 모를 럭비공을 힘차게 찬다

A Living History of Sports and Entertainment

I'm going to dump my sports shoes in the trash.
Shoes which have been my faithful companions,
trainers and close friends for the last five years.

Though we didn't agree on much at first,
gradually we made concessions to each other.

Sometimes these shoes led me to the tennis court in the early morning
or took me to the playground for exercise.
I often trained hard in these shoes.

But on weekends and holidays they guided me to the perfect spot for a picnic
or to the mall for shopping.

When I fell ill they took me to the theater
to experience a living history of sports and entertainment.

Over time I felt these shoes
causing a strange imbalance in my body.

I discovered the bottom soles were worn irregularly.
Perhaps it was time for me to leave them.

It is regretful, but I had to abandon them.
Is there anything that does not grow old in this world?

스포츠와 연예의 산 역사

나는 내 스포츠 신발을
쓰레기통에 버리려고 한다
지난 5년간 나의 충실한 동반자였고
트레이너였고 가까운 친구였던 신발

처음에는 서로 의견이 잘 맞지 않았지만
조금씩 서로 양보를 했다

때로는 이 신발을 신고 아침 일찍 테니스장에
가기도 했고 운동을 하러 운동장에도 갔다
나는 자주 이 신발을 신고 열심히 운동했다

그러나 주말이나 휴일 때면 소풍에 알맞은
장소로 이 신발을 신고 가거나
쇼핑몰에 가서 쇼핑을 했다

병이 나면 나는 이 신발을 신고 스포츠와
연예의 산 역사를 경험하기 위해 극장에 갔다

세월이 흐르면서 나는 이 신발이 내 몸에
이상한 불균형을 가져온다는 것을 느꼈다

나는 신발 굽이 고르게 닳지 않는다는
것을 발견했다 아마도 내가 그 신발을
버려야 할 때가 온 것이리라

애석하지만 나는 그 신발을 버려야한다
이 세상에 나이 들면 늙지 않는 것이 있을까

Filing Cabinet

A rusty filing cabinet stands in the corner of my office.
The painting worn off, discolored.
The door is loosened, the doorknob twisted.
I have used it for more than twenty years,
even as a young businessman.

When she first came to my office
this model was new,
smart, and very smooth
each time I opened the door.
I was the only man to open her.

Nobody knew
the combination, but me.
I trusted the cabinet
with all kinds
of valuable documents.

Every day I opened and
closed it
repeatedly.

Sometimes I slept
in the office
all night with it.

I took my food and coffee
with the cabinet
nearby.

With my expanding business
other filing cabinets came into the office.

They were more colorful, fashionable
with modern functions and safety devices.

파일 캐비닛

녹슨 파일 캐비닛이 내 사무실 한쪽 구석에 있다
칠은 벗겨지고 탈색되었다
문은 헐렁해지고 손잡이는 틀어졌다
내가 젊은 날 사업을 시작한 이래
20년 이상 사용했다

처음 그걸 내 사무실에 들여놓았을 때는
새 것이며 산뜻하고 매우 부드러워
나만이 그 문을 열고 닫았다

캐비닛 비밀번호는 나만 알고 있었고
소중한 서류는 모두 그 속에 넣어두었다

나는 그걸 매일
반복해서 열고 닫았다

때로는 그것과 함께
사무실에서 잠을 자기도 했다

그것 옆에서 식사를 하고
커피를 마셨다

사업이 커지면서 새로운 캐비닛들을
사무실로 들여왔는데

이것들은 더 화려하고 유행을 따른 것들로
현대적 기능과 안전장치를 갖추고 있었다

These new features—
so convenient and useful.

The battered cabinet became a place
merely for storing old documents.

Years later I forgot the combination.
I tried many times to open the drawers, to no avail.

It felt like rock. The door stayed firmly closed.
Until it was forced opened by a locksmith.

새 캐비닛들은 참 편리하고
유용한 게 특징이다

낡은 캐비닛은 옛날 서류들을
보관하는 장소가 되었다

세월이 흘러 나는 그것의
비밀번호를 잊어버렸다
서랍을 열려고 애를 써 보았지만
소용이 없었다.

바위처럼 단단해 열리지 않았다
캐비닛 문은 굳게 닫혀 있었고 결국에는
자물쇠 수리공이 와서
강제로 열 수밖에 없었다

The Black Stone Mermaid:
Is Life the Dream of Dreams?

*There was a virgin, pure of heart, who was planning to marry a young man
who worked on the newly formed crew of the RMS Titanic.
The ship was on its maiden voyage, traveling from England to New York.*

The port was clear as glass.
So smooth it was calm.
Truly that hour never had a sinister feeling
when he departed for New York.
The biggest ship ever built was cheered.
Merrily voyaged on her maiden journey.

Is life the dream of dreams?

But all dreams had vanished into the deep sea
as pieces of the ship crumbled.
Pieces of fantastic times.
Ecstatic days.

Yearning to lose herself in unattainable love
she didn't believe the news.
Couldn't believe in it.
Never admitted it.

"Fiancé never die, we are dreaming only.
The dream will be over very soon."

Is life the dream of dreams?

Though love has gone
memories remain.
Love stories don't fade.
She strongly held that
her fiancé would be coming back soon.
Of course.

검은 돌 인어: 인생이란 꿈을 꾸는 것인가?

여객선 타이타닉에 새 승무원으로 탑승하는 남성과
마음이 순수한 어떤 처녀가 결혼을 앞두고 있었다
배는 영국을 출발하여 뉴욕으로 처녀 출항을 했다

항구는 유리처럼 맑았다
바다는 매끄럽고 잔잔했다
그가 뉴욕을 향해 출발했을 때 불길한 느낌은
전혀 들지 않았다
사람들은 사상 최대의 선박에 환호했다
처녀항해를 기분 좋게 하고 있었다

인생이란 꿈을 꾸는 것인가?

배가 산산조각으로 부서질 때
모든 꿈은 깊은 바다 속으로 사라졌다
화려했던 시절도 황홀했던 날들도…

못 다 이룬 사랑을 이루고 싶은 염원이
너무나 컸기에 그녀는 난파소식을 믿지 않았다
믿을 수 없었다 인정하지 않았다

"피앙세는 결코 죽지 않아.
우리는 단지 꿈을 꾸고 있을 뿐이야
꿈은 금방 끝날 거야."

인생이란 꿈을 꾸는 것인가?

사랑은 떠나가도 추억은 남는 것
사랑의 이야기는 사라지지 않거늘
그녀는 그녀 피앙세가 당연히 금방 돌아올 거라 주장했다

Must be coming back. No doubt in her mind.
"Where is your vow? Give me back my heart."

What is the yearning?
Is it a mist that appears for a little while
then just fades away?
Is it the dream of dreams for a moment?

From morning till evening.
Day to day.
Each month,
every year
of her life.

She sits at the beach
scans the horizon.
Waits for her fiancé.
Calls his name repeatedly.
No longer eats or sleeps.

Still there is no answer,
"Give me back my love, my heart!"

In silence and tears.
In silence and tears.
This yearning for unattainable love
burnt her heart.
The lovely body grew dark and blackened.

Sometime later she became a black stone.
Resembled a mermaid.
Left the world.

What is the yearning?
Is it a mist that appears for a little while
then vanishes like smoke?

Is life the dream of dreams?

그녀는 마음속으로 그녀의 피앙세는 반드시 돌아올 거라
믿었다
"그대의 언약은 어디에 있나요? 나에게 내 마음을
돌려줘요."

그리움은 무엇인가?
그것은 안개처럼 잠깐 나타났다 금방 사라지는 것인가?
그것은 잠깐 꿈을 꾸는 것인가?

어느 한 해도 빠지지 않고 그녀는 아침부터 저녁까지
날이면 날마다 달이면 달마다

바닷가에 앉아 수평선을 응시하며 그녀의 피앙세를
기다린다
더 이상 먹지도 않고 자지도 않고 그의
이름을 부르고 또 부르지만

아무런 대답이 없다
"그대여, 내 사랑을 돌려줘요!"

적막 속에 흘러내리는 눈물, 눈물...
이룰 수 없는 사랑에 대한 갈망은 그녀의 가슴을
태워버렸다
아름답던 육체는 어둡고 까맣게 변해버렸다

얼마 후 그녀는 인어를 닮은 까만 돌이 되어
세상을 떠났다

그리움이란 무엇인가?
그것은 잠깐 동안 안개처럼 나타났다가
연기처럼 사라지는 것인가?

인생이란 꿈을 꾸는 것인가?

Wasted Tire

In the corner of the sequestered village lies an abandoned tire.
Partially covered with once red, now blackened fallen leaves.
While the faint beams of sunset are lazing among the dropped leaves
the breeze blows in and more dried leaves descend.

An old man waiting for a bus looks at this scene for some time.
His forehead is lined with deep furrows
as he thinks dearly of the days gone by.

Now he runs with all his might toward the road ahead.
Like a slave who was kept well under the speed
in order not to be overtaken with the need to dash and scurry
like waves on the shore.

All his life he did his best, with these impediments.
But he couldn't keep the balance
of the time and tide.

That wasted tire might be thinking about speed it had known.
Remembering that speed is all of life.
Or it might be thinking for once in its life about resting awhile.

This day with its freedom from the snare,
it is comfortable with the leaves and breeze,
and its furrows are made smooth by the sunset's beams,
the way the old man's face is made serene with memories of long ago.

폐타이어

격리된 마을 한구석에 폐타이어가 한 개 놓여있다
한때는 붉었지만 이제는 까맣게 변한 낙엽들이
타이어 일부를 덮고 있다
낙엽들 위에는 여린 햇살이 한가롭고
산들바람에 더 많은 낙엽이 떨어진다

버스를 기다리는 노인이 이 장면을 잠시 바라본다
옛 시절을 그리는 이마에는 깊은 주름이 새겨져 있다

해변의 파도처럼 서둘러 돌진해야 하는 필요에
따라 잡히지 않도록 속도를 잘 지켜온 노예처럼
이제 그는 온 힘을 다해 앞으로 달려나간다

이런 장애를 무릅쓰고 그는 평생 최선을
다했지만 세월과 균형을 맞출 수 없었다

폐타이어는 속도가 그의 삶의 전부라는 걸 기억하고
그가 알았던 속도에 대해 생각하거나 그의 일생에
한번 잠깐 휴식을 취한다고 생각할 것이다

오늘 덫에서 벗어나 자유로워졌기에
산들바람 속 낙엽에 파묻혀 있는 것이 편안하다
타이어에 파여진 홈은 노인의 얼굴이 옛날을
그리며 평온해진 것처럼 햇살 속에 매끄럽다

There Were Good Times Too

At the corner of New York City's Central Park,
Michael sets his fatigued body on some old newspapers,
with furrowed, unwashed face he looks down.

His comeliness gone.
His body bent and
drawn over ill-fitting attire.

Once, like others, he had a wife and home.
But now he has only a feeble body
and nightmares each evening.

To try and care for this weakened form he gets a meal sometimes.
He tries his best to survive in this strange land.
Making a livelihood to assimilate in this American society, but in vain.

After tasting life's sweetness,
now all is bitter.
Fallen into homelessness, this night he speaks.

"Hey, Michael, I am sorry.
You have always done well by me,
but what can I do?

You know well that sometimes there were good seasons.
Now I cannot do anything for you, not even offer a scrap of food
or any of those things you need.

I think I would rather go back to the homeland than suffer disgrace.
Then we may forsake hunger for freedom.
What do you think, my lovely body?"

좋은 시절도 있었지

마이클은 뉴욕 센트럴 파크 한쪽에
낡은 신문지를 깔고 그 위에 지친 몸을 누였다
깊게 주름진 씻지도 않은 얼굴로
자신의 몸을 내려다본다

단정했던 그의 모습은 사라지고 없다
구부정한 몸에 잘 맞지도 않은 옷을 걸치고 있다

한때는 그에게 아내도 있었고 집도 있었다
그러나 이제는 그에게 허약한 몸만 남았고
매일 밤 악몽에 시달린다

그는 허약해진 몸을 생각해 가끔씩 식사를 한다
이국 땅에서 살아남으려 미국사회에서 생계를 꾸려보려
최선을 다 했지만 아무 소용없었다

삶의 달콤함을 맛보기도 했지만
이제는 모든 게 쓰기만 하다
노숙자가 된 그가 오늘밤 말한다

"미안해 마이클, 너는 항상 내 곁에서 잘 해 왔지만
정작 내가 할 수 있는 건 뭐지?

너도 알다시피 좋은 시절도 있었지.
그러나 이제는 음식 한 입, 필요한 물건
어느 것 하나 네게 줄 수 없으니
나는 네 은혜를 갚을 길이 없어

망신당하며 사느니 차라리 고향에 가야할까 봐
그러면 배고픔 때문에 자유를 포기하는 게 되겠지
나의 사랑스런 몸이여, 네 생각은 어때?"

Noise Control

A cargo truck ascends the steep rain-sopped road in heat-steamy weather.
The numbing noise of it hangs in the air
pushing on the trucks in front and behind it....

The truck is very slow and patched up looking—ugly.
But its speed is consistent.

Noise from the other trucks seem to add different colors
to its pushing power...
but in vain, the truck moves slowly still.

To escape the noisiness
some people block their ears or close their eyes.
Others leave quite quickly.

Under the shade of a tree—a free zone of quiet—
elders are discussing the luxury car
and appreciating the cicadas' singing.

The sweltering heat comes again and again more frequently,
and the truck's speed has not changed a bit.

소음통제

화물트럭 한 대가 찌는 듯한 더위에
비에 젖은 가파른 길을 오르고 있다
트럭 앞뒤에서 나는 소음을
해결할 도리가 없다

트럭은 아주 느리고 보기 흉하지만
속도는 일정하다

다른 트럭들에서 나는 소음이 그 트럭의
추진력에 새로운 색깔을 더해보지만
아무 소용없고 트럭은 여전히 느릴 뿐이다

소음을 피하기 위해 일부 사람들은 귀를 막거나
눈을 감고 다른 사람들은 재빨리 떠나버린다

나무그늘아래 소음이 없는 안전한 곳에서
어른들은 매미소리를 들으며
고급승용차에 대해 토론하고 있다

찌는 더위가 점점 더 해 가도
트럭의 속도는 조금도 변함이 없다

Secluded Life

I live in a deep valley where there is no telephone,
no television, no computer.
No incoming news ... only the sounds
of sparrows and mountain streams.

I sit on a tree branch or a boulder,
dipping my feet in a stream,
and recall past days.
Yet surveying all I have toiled to achieve
everything seems meaningless.

Once I followed after rainbows,
chased after the wind.
I no longer struggle to exist, now.
I enjoy a life of seclusion
with Nature as my
neighbor.

When I miss my friends,
I go down to the post office and send a letter;
then return to my nest—
singing together with unidentified birds
and playing a game of hide-and-seek
with fawns in the forest.

은둔의 삶

나는 전화도 없고 텔레비전도 없고
컴퓨터도 없는 깊은 계곡에 산다
뉴스도 알 필요 없이 오직 참새소리와
개울물 흐르는 소리만 들리는 곳에서

때로는 나뭇가지나 바위에 앉거나 두발을
개울물에 담그고 지난날을 조용히 회상한다
내가 달성하고자 힘들게 고생했던 모든 것들을
회상해 보니 모두가 다 부질없어 보인다

한때는 나도 무지개를 따라갔고
바람을 쫓아 가보았다
그러나 나는 더 이상 생존을 위해
발버둥치고 싶지 않다
나는 자연을 이웃삼아
은둔의 삶을 만끽하고 있다

내가 계곡에 살다가 친구들이 그리워지면
우체국으로 내려가 편지를 보내고
한가로이 내 보금자리로 돌아와
이름 모를 새들과 함께 노래하고
어린 사슴들과 숲에서 숨바꼭질을 할 것이다

Handwritten Letter

I wrote a handwritten letter to a dear old friend
who lives in the rural village of my homeland.

Over the past several years, I have sent only e-mails,
so now handwriting feels unfamiliar to me.

I place the letter in an envelope;
try to write his name and address on it.

At that moment, mountain brooks flow from my pen;
sparrows fly up and I hear the songs of the birds.

My study becomes the orchard hut; the farmland covered in green,
apricot pink blooms, plum blossoms, ripe cherries and apples.

In the heat of summer, the sound of thunder and bolts of lightning come;
In the fall, farmers store up grains in the barns for later.

Snowy winter comes,
then spring follows.
Even as the seasons change repeatedly,
our friendship is deepened.

I remove the letter from the envelope
and add a lyric he likes to the last line.

At the post office I quietly recall his name again,
and drop the letter into the mailbox.

손으로 쓴 편지

나는 내 시골 마을 고향에 살고 있는
정든 친구에게 손으로 편지를 쓴다

지난 수년 동안 나는 이메일로만 편지를
썼기 때문에 손으로 편지를 쓰려니 어색하다

나는 편지를 봉투에 집어넣고
그의 이름과 주소를 쓰려고 한다

그 순간 산 속 개울물이 나의 펜에서 흐른다
참새들이 날아오르고 내 귀에는
새들의 노랫소리가 들린다

나의 서재는 과수원 오두막이 되고
농지는 초록으로 덮이고 분홍 살구꽃과
자두 꽃이 피어나고 체리와 사과가 무르익는다

무더운 여름에는 번개가 치고 천둥소리가 들린다
가을에는 농부들이 장래를 대비해
곡식을 헛간에 저장한다

눈 내리는 겨울이 오면 봄이 뒤따른다
계절은 자꾸 변해가지만
친구와의 우정은 깊어만 간다

나는 봉투에서 편지를 꺼내 친구가 좋아하는
시 한 편을 편지 마지막 줄에 첨가한다

우체국에서 나는 친구의 이름을 다시 한번
상기한 다음 편지를 우편함에 넣는다

My Father Is With Me

My father passed away a long time ago.
But he is still with me.
He never went to school.
But knew everything.
He knew what love was.

I loved my father like he loved me.
He was neither rich nor proud.
Never said to do good.
But did good works always.

My father knew the way to fix trust.
And keep it.
He knew the right way to sail through life's journey.

When I went astray in my life
he told me, "There is nothing you cannot do."

My father was not a doctor,
but he healed the sickness of my body and mind.
When I grew weak,
he trained and disciplined me.

My father has passed away.
But he is in my heart as a master compass.
My soul is always steeped in joy with him.
In his breast I sleep,
dreaming in the sound
his breathing kept,
and in the surging crowd,
toiling, striving from day to day.

Knowing whatever happens,
my father is with me.

나와 함께 하는 나의 아버님

나의 아버님은 오래전에 작고하셨다
그럼에도 아버님은 아직도 나와 함께 계신다
아버님은 학교를 다닌 적이 없지만 모든 걸 아셨다
아버님은 사랑이 무엇인지 아셨다

아버님께서 날 사랑하셨던 것처럼
나도 아버님을 사랑했다
아버님은 부유하지도 교만하지도 않으셨다
좋은 일을 한다고 말씀은 안 하시지만
항상 좋은 일을 하셨다

아버님은 신뢰를 쌓는 방법을 아셨고
그 방법을 지키셨다
아버님은 삶의 여정을 헤쳐 나가는
법을 제대로 알고 계셨다

내가 살면서 길을 잃을 때 아버님께서는
"네가 할 수 없는 일은 이 세상에 없다." 라고
말씀해 주신다

아버님은 의사는 아니셨지만
내 몸과 마음의 병을 치유해 주셨다
내가 허약해질 때면 아버님께서는
나를 훈련시키고 훈육해 주셨다

아버님은 떠나가셨지만 아버님은
내 가슴에 남아 나침반 역할을 해 주신다
내 영혼은 언제나 아버님과 함께 하는
기쁨에 젖어 있다
나는 아버님 품안에서 잠이 들어
아버님 숨소리를 들으며 꿈을 꾼다
그리고 몰려드는 군중들 틈에서
나날이 분투노력한다

무슨 일이 있더라도
아버님은 나와 함께 하신다

The Train Passes

The train passes along the Hudson River,
Its whistle heard all along the riverside.
If there were no whistles in this city, how prosaic life would be.

Every time the train goes by, the river's waves lick about the ships,
drowsy flowers beside the bank awaken from their midday nap,
and people turn to brooding and imagining the places they might be carried.

The train is bringing the passengers and their dreams
together with my empty mind;
passing by the riverbank, the open field and across the country.

The train is puffing away along the railroad,
where the green signal lamp beckons.
The train passes by the autumn forest and the dark shadows pass over.
My mind follows them aimlessly.

기차가 지나간다

허드슨강을 따라 기차가 지나간다
강변을 따라 내내 기적을 울린다
이 도시에 기적소리가 없다면 얼마나 따분할까

기차가 지나갈 때마다 강물의 파도가 뱃전에 부서지고
강둑에 핀 꽃들은 대낮의 낮잠에서 깨어나고
사람들은 그들이 가게 될지도 모를 장소에 대해
숙고하고 상상도 한다

기차는 승객들과 그들의 꿈과 나의 공허한 마음을 싣고
강둑을 지나 넓은 들판을 지나 국토를 횡단한다

기차는 철길을 따라 녹색등이 손짓하는 곳으로
가쁜 숨을 내쉬며 달려간다
기차가 가을 숲을 지나자 어두운 그림자들도 지나가고
내 마음은 그것들을 정처 없이 따라간다

While Changing the Calendar

While I exchange last year's calendar for a new one
days flit through my mind like moving pictures.

Many days have vanished; where are they?
When did they leave me?

It isn't easy to remember the days,
even though I think back or look deeply into history.

Now, I turn the faded calendar
and memories return.

The days jumping over other days,
just as I fold the months back again.

On a certain day, some people throw a stone,
some cast a net, and some sing a song.
Now all of them have gone.

While opening this year's calendar I tell myself:
"An old year has gone and a new one has come.
I begin again toward my happy dream."

달력을 바꾸면서

작년 달력을 새것으로 바꾸는 동안
세월이 활동사진처럼
내 마음을 스쳐 지나간다

많은 날들이 사라졌는데
그들은 모두 어디로 갔나?
언제 나를 떠나갔나?

뒤를 돌아봐도
역사를 깊이 들여다봐도
떠나간 날들을 기억할 수 없다

이제 빛 바랜 달력을 넘기니
기억이 돌아온다

지나간 달들을 다시 접다 보니
특별했던 날들은 다른 날들보다
먼저 생각난다

어떤 날들에는 일부사람들이 돌을 던졌고
일부는 그물을 던졌고 일부는 노래를 불렀지만
그들은 이제 모두 갔다

새해 달력을 펴면서 묵은해가 가고
새해가 왔으니 나의 행복한 꿈을 향해
다시 시작하자고 스스로 다짐을 한다

About the Author and the Translator

Han-Jae Lee has studied poetry at Chung-Ang University and Korea University, and in the United States at library workshops in Santa Cruz, San Jose and at the Hudson Valley Writers' Center in New York. In 2005 his poem, "A High-rise Apartment," won a silver award in a national contest sponsored by The National Assembly of Korea and The Federation of Korean Cultural Center. His first poetry collection, *A High-rise Apartment*, was published in Korea in 2008. He also co-published three poetry anthologies, and his poems have appeared in several Korean literary magazines. His debut collection in English, *The Golden Gate Bridge and Other Natural Wonders*, was published by River Sanctuary Publishing in 2013. His chapbook, *A Place Where Clouds Are Flowing*, was published by Finishing Line Press in 2017. His third collection, *Korea My Homeland*, was published by Finishing Line Press in 2019. Lee's poems have appeared in *Catamaran Literary Reader*, *Monterey Poetry Review*, *Caesura*, *Sand Hill Review*, *Crab Orchard Review*, *PCC Inscape Magazine*, *Military Experience & The Arts*, *Snapdragon Journal*, and *EMRYS Journal*.

Translator Jae-Mo Lee graduated from Korea University in 1978, majoring in English Literature. In 2011 he was recognized as one of the five new poets of the year by Seorabeol Art New Entertainment in Seoul, Korea. In the same year, a selection of his poems was published by Evergreen Publishing Corporation in Korea. In 2012, a selection of modern Korean poems he translated into English was published by the same publisher.